MAKING SPACE FOR
FORMATION

CON

TENTS

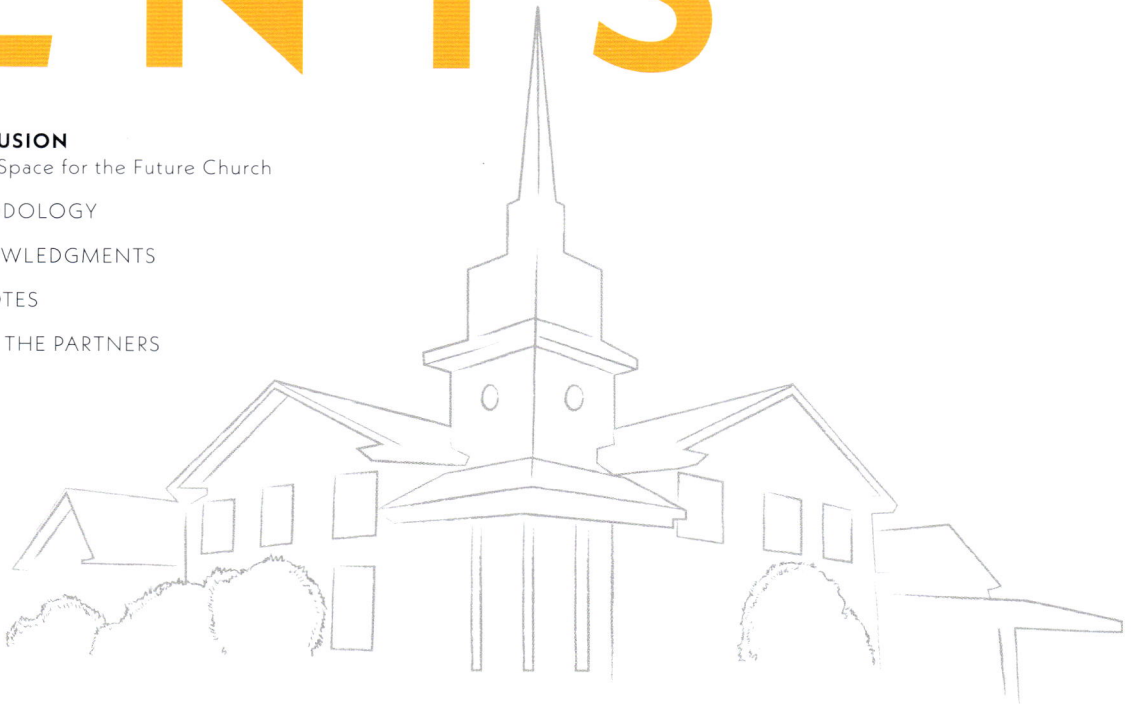

Church Buildings Cast a Vision of Who God Is

At Aspen Group, we've recently started using language surrounding "building a better future for the church." We believe that, as Winston Churchill once said, "We shape our buildings; thereafter our buildings shape us."

Churches have been the center of communities, thought of as a place of great power and a place of literal refuge for the poor and needy. They have been built in cruciform shapes to remind Christians of the cross of Jesus and with steeples and bell towers to stand out in the community. Some have sanctuaries while others have worship centers. Some house incredible art while others double as preschools or coffee shops. Some are Gothic, some are classical, some are modern, some are institutional.

Just as the church building has shown up in different ways throughout history, these sacred spaces speak to people in uniquely different ways. Church buildings help cast a vision of who God is— his goodness, his beauty and his desires for our lives. As designers, it is our responsibility to uphold this meaning and make sure it is expressed in a church space.

When we embarked on this research journey with Barna, we had two hopes in mind. First, we wanted to test some intuitions we had about how spaces affect people. One of the hardest things to do in our work of designing and building church spaces is to communicate (and help pastors communicate) the value of certain design decisions.

I remember several years ago trying to convince a church not to remove a large monument fireplace out of the scope of their lobby redesign. The piece was pricey and, as they faced budget challenges, it seemed like the most obvious thing to cut.

At the time, all I could say was, "Just trust me." But that doesn't help a pastor who is trying to generate support among the congregation. Years later while visiting the site, the pastor said to me, "I get it now." As people engaged in the space, that fireplace served as a point of interest and comfort for conversation and connection—and the value and meaning of a once obscure design element became clear. *This* is what the *Making Space* series is about: helping leaders see the intersection of space and spirituality.

Second, with this research we hoped to create something that equips pastors for ministry. Venturing into a building project is high-stakes leadership, and pastors need words and wisdom to communicate the intention behind key decisions.

We often work with healthy, growing congregations looking for solutions to problems that have come from their growth like not having enough seats in worship, needing more classes for kids' ministry or dealing with congestion in the lobby. However, **well-built church spaces don't just solve problems; they shape your church's culture**. Church spaces speak a language without words (for better or worse), and this is something we have the power to shape through intentional design.

I hope and pray that this final journal, alongside volumes 1 and 2, will inspire pastors and church leaders to look at their buildings differently, thinking about how small details contribute to a more human feeling, how a grand space can help visitors feel less anxious because it puts them in physical contrast to an all-powerful God and how visual beauty can remind us of the splendor and goodness of God.

As a company, we can commit to building a better future for the church not because of our efforts, but because God himself has already guaranteed a better future for *his Church*. Scripture reminds us that "he who began a good work in you will bring it to completion at the day of Jesus Christ"

(Philippians 1:6). Ephesians 5:27 promises he will "present the church to himself as a radiant church, without stain or wrinkle or any other blemish, but holy and blameless." And in Matthew 16:17–19, Jesus assures even the gates of hell will not prevail against his Church.

I'm so proud of this resource created in partnership with the Barna team. It's been encouraging to see their enthusiasm for this project grow with each volume. I personally hope that the design of this journal, the beautiful and thoughtful illustrations and the intentionality behind each word, will inspire you with a new imagination for what is possible.

Making Space for Formation provides more direct suggestions and ideas for how you might make space in your church. From the Q&As and "Think on This" sections, to notes "From the Architect" throughout, I pray that it will help you, as Barna says, understand the times and know what to do (1 Chronicles 12:32). ●

DEREK DEGROOT
Aspen Group
President

INTRODUCTION BY

BARNA GROUP

Today, we are in the midst of another shift.

The Millennials who stayed in the Church are now the rising pastors and leaders. Gen Z, the most diverse, cause-driven generation, are finding their place—and holding churches and leaders accountable.

Culturally, the world is turning toward secularism, individualism, consumerism and general distrust of Christian leaders. Yet there's also opportunity for the Church to uniquely show up to counter prevalent feelings of loneliness, anxiety and lack of purpose.

> **In a world that is distancing itself relationally from the Church, a respect and reverence for the physical church building remain**

Barna first connected with Aspen Group, our partners for this *Making Space* series, in 2015 for research surrounding the needs and desires of Millennials. At that time, as church leaders struggled to understand the emerging generation, Barna was immersed in studying Millennials. Our research revealed that churches were largely failing to reach and retain young adults, leading many Christian Millennials to leave the Church altogether.[1]

Anticipating the far-reaching implications of this exodus, Barna and Aspen set out to learn what factors in churches might help young people better connect with God and remain in faith community. That research, *Making Space for Millennials,* helped leaders begin to see the potential ministry impact of creating space—both literal and figurative—at such a pivotal time for the Church.

Today's society calls for relevant ministry, authentic leadership and—whether we realize it or not—meaningful spaces. Busy, overstimulated minds need a place of respite and clarity. Weary, lost souls need space to feel comfort and belonging.

Aspen Group has remained dedicated to honoring the church as more than a building, as a place where biblical principles and practices are built into the character of each room. That's why we're working together again to widen the net on the subject of church design, looking at ways Christian beliefs and faith practices are influenced by space—and why understanding them is so crucial in these times.

Formational Spaces

In a digital world connected through smart devices and social media and, increasingly, shaped by artificial intelligence, the physical realm can seem less relevant. But Barna research shows otherwise.

Most U.S. adults still value in-person encounters over alternative options.[2] And Christian or not, they widely view the church as a sacred space that should be set apart in its community. Even in a world that is distancing itself relationally from the Church, respect and reverence for the physical church building remain and should not be ignored.

Barna data also shows that one of the biggest concerns within churches is the crucial area of discipleship. In *Growing Together*, we revealed that two in five Christians (39%) aren't engaged in discipleship community at all.[3] During and following the pandemic, many pastors have struggled with how best to retain members, help them grow spiritually and equip them for mission.

The *Making Space* project has unveiled growing opportunities for church buildings to bridge the discipleship gap.

In volume 1 of this series, *Making Space for Inspiration*, we explained how peace and calm produce the quiet moments needed to draw people toward feelings of spirituality or transcendence. This report set the foundation to better understand the characteristics of certain spaces and how people commonly interact with them.

Volume 2, *Making Space for Community*, showed how church can be a natural, uniquely valuable place for people to reflect, interact, be inspired and build relationships on Sunday and beyond. But there are big responsibilities that come with making space for people to commune with God and others. People expect the church building to reflect care and concern for both community and congregants.

Making Space for Formation is the culmination of this trilogy, and, we hope, the most galvanizing.

You'll likely notice a theme of vision-casting in this report. That's because meaningful space requires vision, a set plan and purpose. And that vision requires leadership, well-informed and intentional.

Previous volumes in this series showed the power space can have in shaping people's behaviors and experiences. Now it's time to create a plan to make space in your church, and ultimately for the spiritual development of those who enter.

GLOSSARY

Generations:

- **Gen Z:** Born between 1999 and 2015 *(The sample for this study only includes Gen Z adults born between 1999 and 2004.)*

- **Millennial:** Born between 1984 and 1998

- **Gen X:** Born between 1965 and 1983

- **Boomer:** Born between 1946 and 1964

Faith Affiliation:

- **Self-identified Christians:** Those who self-identify as Christian or with a Christian denomination.

- **Practicing Christians:** Those who self-identify as Christian, agree strongly that faith is very important in their lives and have attended church within the past month.

- **Nonpracticing Christians:** Self-identified Christians who do not qualify as practicing.

- **Non-Christians:** U.S. adults who do not identify as Christian.

INTRODUCING A SPECTRUM OF SPIRITUAL ENGAGEMENT

Spiritual formation is a multifaceted term used to describe the process of growing closer to God. In this journal, we'll talk about some of the practices, behaviors and circumstances that might aid in a Christian's formation. Recognizing that there's no single definition of "spiritual formation" that applies across all denominations, traditions and contexts Barna is studying, you'll also find insights from contributors (see page 14 for a list of contributors), including experts and scholars who have written on the subject, giving a robust view of what spiritual formation can look like.

To help church leaders better envision the impact of formational spaces, we've also created a custom segmentation based on a set of questions related to a respondent's spiritual beliefs and faith practices. This "**spectrum of spiritual engagement**" gauges where a Christian is in their faith journey from "devoted" to "disengaged." For the purpose of this study, a "devoted" Christian is one who:

- Strongly agrees, "My religious faith is important in my life."

Barna's Spectrum of Spiritual Engagement

Devoted answer yes to all three	**Engaged** answer yes to two	**Growing** answer yes to one	**Disengaged** answer yes to none

Spiritual Engagement by Generation

Base: Christians

● Devoted ● Engaged ● Growing ● Disengaged

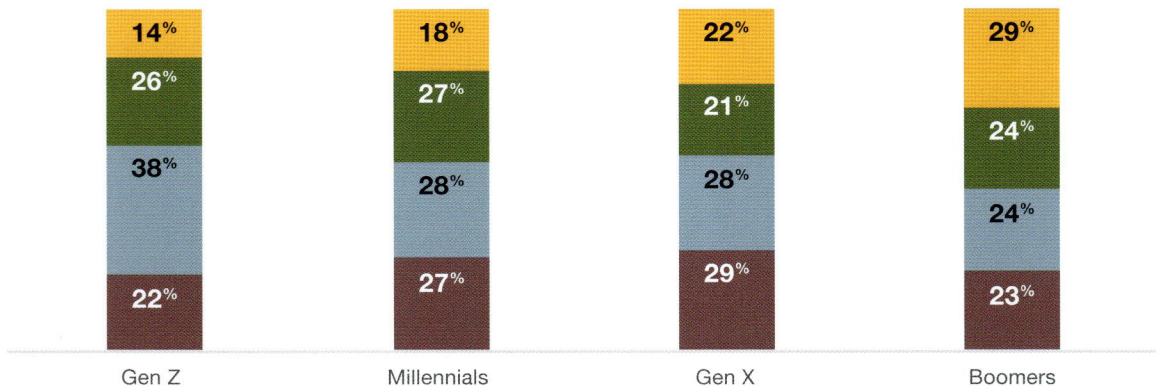

	Gen Z	Millennials	Gen X	Boomers
Disengaged	14%	18%	22%	29%
Growing	26%	27%	21%	24%
Engaged	38%	28%	28%	24%
Devoted	22%	27%	29%	23%

n=1,203 U.S. adult Christians, February 28–March 9, 2022.

- Strongly agrees, "Jesus was crucified and raised from the dead to conquer sin and death."
- Says "yes" they are currently being discipled.

From there, the spectrum describes a Christian as either "engaged" (a self-identified Christian who meets two of the three above statements), "growing" (a self-identified Christian who meets one of them) or "disengaged" (a self-identified Christian who does not meet any of the above statements). We'll view the research through this lens to better understand ways physical space may influence a Christian's perspectives and behaviors.

Of course, there are many factors that contribute to a person's faith journey and how their faith is lived out. There will, no doubt, be observations in the data that perhaps don't apply to your church culture, denomination or needs. **It's best to view this spectrum as informative, not prescriptive.** Try not to jump to conclusions about how a Christian might think or act based on their perceived level of spiritual engagement. The data may reveal insights that are different than what you'd assume.

Our hope is that, as you assess various stages of spiritual engagement, you'll see your own congregants in the research—better understanding their needs, both spiritual and physical, and how your building plays a part. ●

PRINCIPLES OF CHURCH DESIGN

As discussed in the introduction, volume 3 is about helping you cast vision and begin the process of *making space* in your church. With some guidance from our partners at Aspen Group, we put together this list of terms you might hear or think about in your own conversations about church design strategy:

Adaptive reuse: The design process of converting a building that formerly had a different purpose into another use, such as a church.

Biophilia / biophilic design: Used to describe humans' natural affinity for nature and the incorporation of nature or natural materials into architectural design.

Building footprint: The perimeter of a building on the land on which it sits.

Built environment: The human-made and modified structures that comprise the places where we live and work, including roads, civil amenities, landscaping and private buildings.

Conceptual design: The movement of a vision into diagrams that depict the architectural intent of a space.

Design-build: A construction project delivery method in which the owner, architect, contractor and subcontractors work together as one team to build a project.

Flow: The movement of people through a space, including entering, exiting and gathering.

Hospitable space: Spaces that take into consideration the basic needs of the people who engage there, whether that means providing trash cans and water fountains in a park or having a café hand-off that is handicap accessible.

Human-scale design: Environments that are designed for the human body to interact with, based on average human proportions, without assistance from technology or mechanics.

Integrated project delivery: A construction project delivery method that utilizes the talents and insights of all project participants to maximize efficiency and project outcomes. This method is usually highly collaborative since all parties (owner, architect and contractor) are aligned by a single contract.

Massing: The overall size and shape of a building, often laid out in basic geometric shapes (e.g., cubes, cones, pyramids). This is often an early step in master planning and determining the general boundaries of a building.

Modularity: The degree to which components can be rearranged, replaced or separated.

Neighborhood / community fabric: A metaphor to describe the way the physical elements of a community connect, relate and interact. This includes everything from streets and parks to buildings and parking lots.

Placemaking: A term introduced in the 1960s by Jane Jacobs and William H. Whyte to describe the process of creating places that transform public spaces to strengthen the connections between people and the places they share.

Program: The description of a building plan based on the functions and requirements of the space.

Sacred space: A space that is set apart for religious use, using forms, objects and other design elements to make this purpose explicit.

Third place: A term coined by Ray Oldenberg to describe the social spaces, after home and work, where people go to connect with others.

Threshold: A boundary people cross when entering or beginning something. A threshold can be formal, such as the front door of a church or room. A threshold can also be abstract or psychological, such as the entry onto a church property altogether.

Visual clarity: The experience of knowing what is going on and what is expected of a person when they walk into a space. A simple example might be that when a visitor walks into a church lobby, they quickly know (whether by signage or by other intuitive design elements) where to go to the bathroom and where to check their kids into children's ministry.

Wayfinding: The signage that helps people know what is available to them in a space and how to find it. Wayfinding can also include nonverbal signage, such as flooring patterns and other features that provide direction.

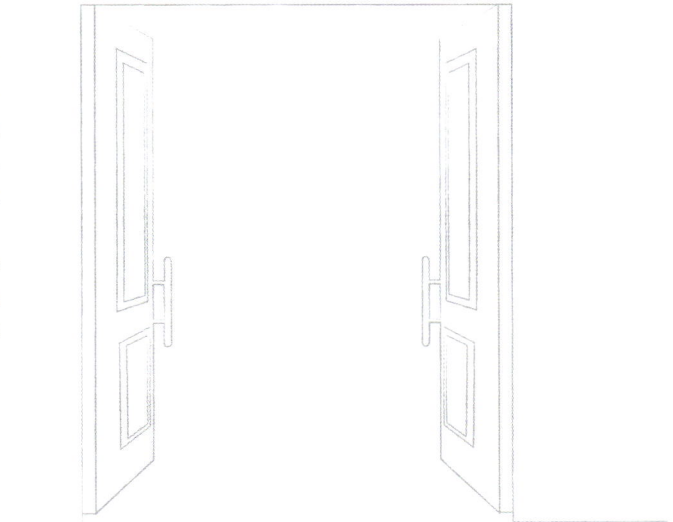

IN THIS VOLUME

Throughout the *Making Space* series, you'll find advice, thoughts and ideas from a diverse group of contributors, including pastors and other church leaders, Bible scholars, professors, authors, architects, designers and creatives with valuable experience related to church design for ministry impact.

Emmanuel Brown
Cofounder &
COO of ChurchSpace

David Deeds
Co-manager of the
Christ Lutheran Church
community garden

Day Edwards
Cofounder & CEO
of ChurchSpace

Al Gordon
Rector of Saint Church

Jessica Gracewski
Associate pastor
at Reality Church,
San Francisco

Elizabeth Howze
Director of teaching,
training & learning at
Ormond Center

Duke Kwon
Lead pastor of Grace
Meridian Hill

Ryan Moody
Landscape architect,
founding principal of
Moody Graham

THE CONVERSATION CONTINUES ON THE *MAKING SPACE* PODCAST, CREATED BY BARNA IN PARTNERSHIP WITH ASPEN GROUP. SCAN TO LISTEN OR VISIT BARNA.COM/MAKINGSPACE.

Matthew Niermann

Associate dean of the College of Architecture, Visual Arts & Design at California Baptist University

Rachel Reed

Church designer

Walt Roth

Co-manager of the Christ Lutheran Church community garden

Michael Scheer

Interim director of the Center for Liturgical Art

Elaine Schnabel

Assistant professor of organizational communication at Weber State University

Heather Sibinski

Pastor, director of building & property teams at Living Word Christian Center

David Taylor

Theologian, author & speaker

Cynthia Wallace

Executive pastor of Bible Center Church

1

UNDERSTAND WHAT'S EXPECTED

So the Word became human and made his home among us. He was full of unfailing love and faithfulness.
And we have seen his glory, the glory of the Father's one and only Son.

JOHN 1:14 (NLT)

Writing in the *Washington Post,* pastor Duke Kwon had this to say as he witnessed church buildings across Washington, D.C., being torn down or converted into condominiums:

> Churches need to be convinced that buildings matter. Followers of Jesus need to recover a theology of place, space and parish that promotes the value of the built environment. [As we] remember Christ's bodily resurrection, [we can] reclaim the historic Christian belief that God cares about physical stuff—bodies and buildings.[4]

The first step of "making space" is to eliminate the assumption that church buildings aren't relevant or needed to make an impact. Jesus "made his home among us," and church buildings are visible reminders of that indwelling.

But church design isn't in the realm of expertise for the average pastor. Leaders may not have a good understanding of what church visitors desire, expect or actually experience in their building—or how these factors might affect a congregant for better or worse.

Spiritual growth and development *do* fall into a pastor's wheelhouse: Pastors want to see people and communities changed by the gospel. So let's look at *church building* transformation from the perspective of *heart* transformation. This is especially important when people are more spiritually open (74% of U.S. adults tell Barna they want to grow spiritually[5]) and perhaps looking for a church to welcome them in.

A Hub for Spiritual Life

As we have noted throughout the *Making Space* series, a core finding of this research is the recognized significance of the church beyond its mere physicality—62 percent of U.S. adults agree the Christian church building is a sacred space. The same percentage of people (62%) consider the Christian church to be transcendent, defined by half of U.S. adults as a place with a "sense of peace and calm."

The church is viewed as a natural place to discuss spiritual matters; 44 percent of U.S. adults say they would feel comfortable having a meaningful conversation about spiritual faith at a Christian church. Many (61%) also say they would be at least "somewhat likely" to visit church if they were feeling introspective.

This should encourage pastors: Christian or not, most people value a church as more than just a

The Church Is Still Sacred

Think about a Christian church building. Which of the following is closer to your personal belief?

- All Christians
- Devoted
- Engaged
- Growing
- Disengaged

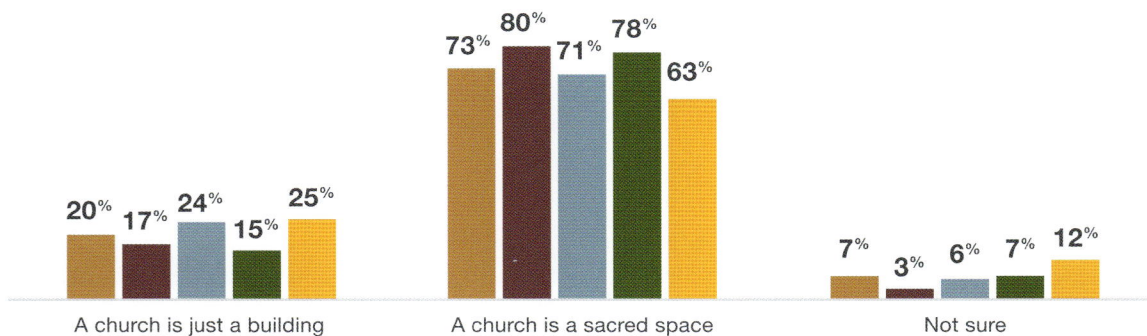

A church is just a building
- All Christians: 20%
- Devoted: 17%
- Engaged: 24%
- Growing: 15%
- Disengaged: 25%

A church is a sacred space
- All Christians: 73%
- Devoted: 80%
- Engaged: 71%
- Growing: 78%
- Disengaged: 63%

Not sure
- All Christians: 7%
- Devoted: 3%
- Engaged: 6%
- Growing: 7%
- Disengaged: 12%

n=1,238 U.S. adult Christians, February 28–March 9, 2022.

In the chart above, you may be curious about the fluctuations in responses among engaged Christians. Though engaged Christians may be thought to be further along in their spiritual journey, they are less certain than growing Christians that the church is a sacred space. While Barna can't say why this manifests in the data, it does remind us that spiritual growth is not always linear. Keep this in mind as you assess where your members are in their spiritual development and how your church might respond.

building, and certain emotions or experiences may draw them *into* the building.

Among Christians, data shows that **connection to the church building deepens with spiritual engagement**. Overall, three in four Christians (73%) say they believe a church is a sacred space, but disengaged Christians (25%) are more likely than devoted and growing Christians to say, "a church is just a building." Disengaged Christians are also more likely than Christians at all other levels of spiritual engagement to be unsure of the church's meaning (12%).

The depth of a Christian's spiritual formation appears to correlate with their understanding of the sacred significance of the church building, perhaps because of what they have experienced in the space themselves. Devoted Christians may be more apt to grasp what the Very Rev. Samuel Candler writes about his church, St. Phillip's Cathedral: "The actual physical place has provided the space for our human struggle to meet divine grace. ... Our cathedral is holy because *holy things have happened here*."[6] As a holy place, the church helps shape how Christians understand their Creator.

"Buildings and other forms of human making shape us [because] our bodies affect our souls as much as our souls affect our bodies," writes Matthew Lee Anderson, founder of Mere Orthodoxy and assistant research professor at Baylor University's Institute for Studies of Religion. "[While Christians] have rightly focused on the interior life, the interior life has a particular shape based on whether and how we 'present [our] bodies' as a living sacrifice. While architecture may not be the main thing for [Christians], the main thing isn't the only thing that matters."[7]

The Church Is "Different"

Most Christians (62%) expect the church building to be "one that stands out and is recognizable as a church in its surrounding community." This

What's Preserved?: Honor Church History, Tradition & Culture

Preserving the roots of your ministry through your church space not only fosters a sense of identity for congregants (by giving them an understanding of what they are a part of), it informs what's taught, practiced, modeled and transmitted.

What do you want your church to be known for? Answer this, then weigh that against how your church is *actually* viewed. Ask congregants for their thoughts on your church's history and culture. Ask neighbors for their thoughts on your church's presence in the community. Pay attention to what's consistently said and desired by those you serve. Then, take what you've learned to the design table.

underscores a common understanding today that **churches aren't meant to blend in**. They are special, holy, set apart.

What, then, is unique about your church building? About your congregation? About your mission? With these answers in mind, consider what is communicated, emphasized and reflected to visitors through your building, inside and out.

Going further, our data reveals that most people (72%) describe their ideal church as "traditional" rather than "trendy" (this was asked of all U.S. adults). This is no knock on the churches that subscribe to more contemporary architecture or practices. The main thing to take from this is that **there's still a place for tradition in church today.** Architectural features like steeples, towers and stained glass have long been associated with church buildings. Even if your church lacks these historically common components, it can be beneficial to incorporate visual elements that distinguish your building from others in your community to say, "This is a church, a place to draw near to God."

A churchgoer in a Barna-led focus group for the *Making Space* project explains it this way: "I notice all this stained glass, and it makes me feel like [I'm] completely separated from the outside world. When I come in here, I feel like I'm in a different place."

Space can transport a person to another state of mind. And in church, this journey can be a transcendent one. Visitors are given an opportunity to remove themselves from worldly distractions, making room for the divine. Ultimately, these experiences can move a person along in their journey to or with God.

The Church Builds Community

Additionally, **church space can uniquely help people form relationships.** Another Barna-led focus group participant, this time a non-Christian, recognized the importance of the church in creating and encouraging community: "I think [a church building] is meant to be more than a church. It's meant to be someplace where you'd go for a sense of community and socialization. [It's not just] a place of worship. You'd come here to see your friends and your neighbors, and your children would become friends with the other children."

Beyond what a church can offer in terms of formal teaching and preaching, the connective and communal elements of church participation cannot be underestimated. The rhythms of church community—weekly worship, monthly prayer nights, quarterly meetings and beyond—all serve as consistent ways to deepen community and encourage formation.

[When thinking about] the buildings that we inhabit—whether you're in a new church or in a church that's been there for [decades or centuries], the first place to start is with the obvious theological point: Jesus really loves people. The buildings are not the [main] thing. But why does God build a temple in the Old Testament? *So that we can encounter him.*

As the body of Christ, as people who follow Jesus, it's all about Jesus. The buildings are collections of atoms and dust. But God does inhabit space. He does care about matter.

As a theologian friend of mine says, "Matter *matters*." [This is important] particularly in a generation like ours that's struggling with what it means to be virtual and what it means to be present. The buildings we have been gifted—whether you are a pastor in a coffee shop plant in downtown Seattle or in a traditional denomination with an old building that's leaking—these buildings and spaces are part of God's plan to love the people who live in that place.

—**Al Gordon**

The Important Historical Roles of Sacred Spaces

Throughout U.S. history, the church building has served an important role for surrounding communities as they both help provide a sense of belonging and encourage the spiritual formation of those who enter.

"Think about the monumental Polish churches built in midwestern cities like Chicago in the late 19th century," Evan Sparks, board member of Sacred Spaces Conservancy, a Washington, D.C.-based non-profit working to preserve religious spaces, tells Barna. "Working class immigrants who were new to this country contributed their labor and savings to craft opulent sanctuaries that provided a taste of the baroque churches in the old country. These buildings didn't just serve as places of worship; they reflected the pride of a community of new Americans and helped them maintain and deepen a connection to the spirituality—and community—of their homeland."

Likewise, throughout the Civil Rights Movement, local church spaces were the hub of Black communities.

"The church was at the center of those communities not only as a safe haven, but a space of formation, a space of worship, a space of education, a space of fellowship, a space of development of young people—not only in terms of spiritual formation but the human formation," explains Rev. Kermit Moss, interim director of the Center for Black Church Studies at Princeton Theological Seminary. "It was an intentional space."[8]

Though individualism is deeply rooted in today's society, Barna research reveals that most Christians value community over privacy at church. Zooming in, devoted Christians in particular believe building strong relationships with other Christians is significantly more important than hearing a thought-provoking sermon (59% vs. 38%, respectively). This isn't a recommendation to preach less, but to take note: **The spiritually mature especially value space to grow their faith *with others.***

For the devoted Christian, this is reflected in their church attendance. Devoted Christians are nearly four times more likely to have attended a Christian church service in the last month compared to disengaged Christians (62% of devoted vs. 16% of disengaged Christians). With greater spiritual engagement come more consistent rhythms of faith practices like churchgoing.

A church provides familiar faces in the same place week after week, and it's through these familiar faces that a churchgoer can be seen and valued. Don't overlook the role your church space plays in building community. Formational experiences like fellowship, friendship, support and accountability all stem from it.

Social connections may be part of the emotional connection that Christians of all engagement levels say matters most to them in church. Across the spectrum of spiritual engagement, Christians emphasize their emotional connection to a church, even over how good a church looks (74% of devoted Christians, 75% of engaged Christians, 70% of growing Christians and 58% of disengaged Christians say having an emotional connection to a church is more important to them than a church that's aesthetically pleasing).

Disengaged & Devoted Christians Value Strong Connections Most

At a Christian church, which of the following is more important to you?

Base: Christians

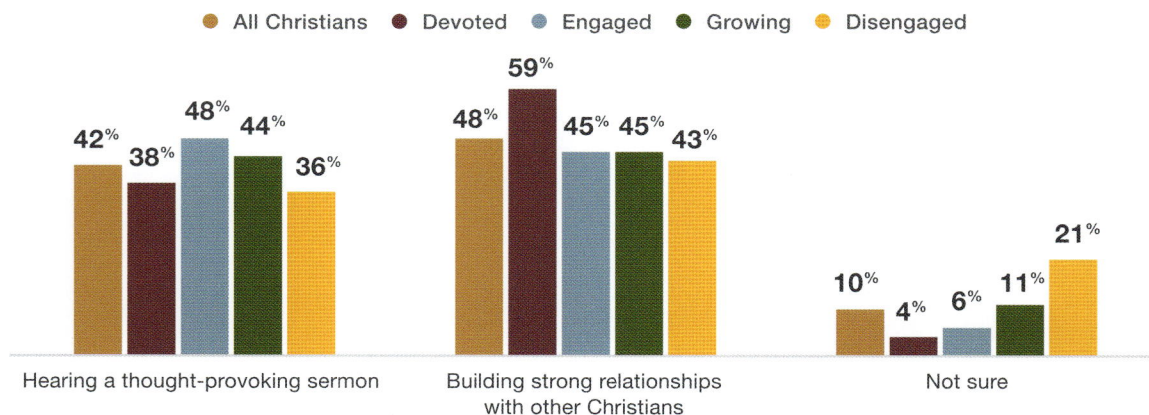

● All Christians ● Devoted ● Engaged ● Growing ● Disengaged

Hearing a thought-provoking sermon: 42%, 38%, 48%, 44%, 36%

Building strong relationships with other Christians: 48%, 59%, 45%, 45%, 43%

Not sure: 10%, 4%, 6%, 11%, 21%

n=1,238 U.S. adult Christians, February 28–March 9, 2022.

This doesn't discount the value of a well-designed church; it amplifies the important role relationships and experiences play in churchgoing. **Your building is a part of the memories (good or bad) visitors form**. In what ways is your church set apart? When visitors enter your building, how does your space help people focus on the sacred nature of the church?

The Church Is for Anyone

The general consensus in this study is that a church isn't just for its members.

Almost all Christians agree (55% strongly, 37% somewhat) that churches have a responsibility to care for their community. As Christians advance in their spiritual engagement, we see higher expectations for how the church is to exist and serve. For instance, three-fourths of devoted Christians (75%) strongly agree with this

statement, compared to just one-third of disengaged Christians (33%).

This could mean that as you focus more on the spiritual formation of your congregants, they will want to see your church engage more in the surrounding community: As Christians are formed, they increasingly care about how others are invited into that formation, too. So how does your church building welcome others—including neighbors who may not know Jesus, may need your help or may be skeptical of the Church?

"God has always wanted the vulnerable in society to be cared for," Bible teacher and civil rights leader John M. Perkins writes in his book *Dream with Me*. "He never intended for them to languish in poverty, abuse, slavery, homelessness or other types of devastation. When we care for individuals who are trapped in these ways, when we show them love and help them move toward freedom and

"Churches Have a Responsibility to Care for Their Community"

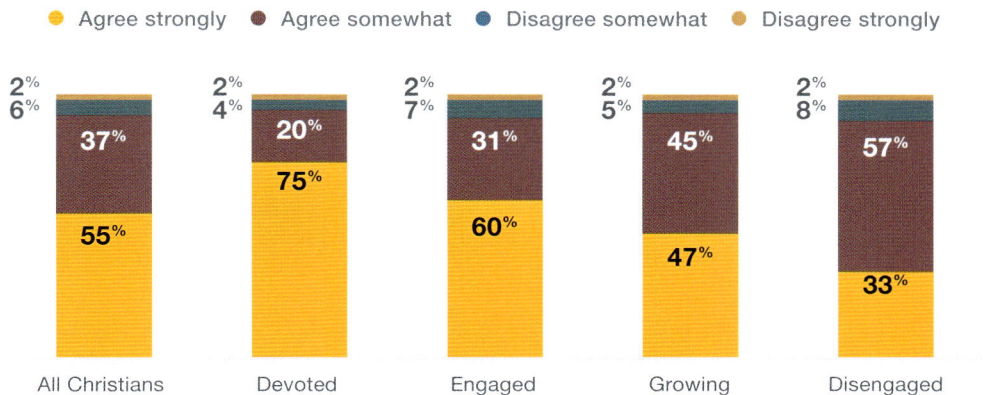

● Agree strongly ● Agree somewhat ● Disagree somewhat ● Disagree strongly

	All Christians	Devoted	Engaged	Growing	Disengaged
Disagree strongly	2%	2%	2%	2%	2%
Disagree somewhat	6%	4%	7%	5%	8%
Agree somewhat	37%	20%	31%	45%	57%
Agree strongly	55%	75%	60%	47%	33%

n=1,238 U.S. adult Christians, February 28–March 9, 2022.

Placemaking is so important to the church [because] everyone is watching the labels we use to describe our church. Even people who don't attend church are interested in whose opinions we listen to, whose needs we address and how we design our churches to meet those needs. How you design your church communicates something about who your church is.

—Elaine Schnabel

wholeness, we participate in bringing a little part of God's Kingdom back into alignment with his greater plan. We do justice and God smiles."[9]

Christians caring for others is participation in Church mission, and through this, God is known more deeply. This care can be expressed as hospitality and outreach through your church building or property. Service to your community will probably require work outside of Sunday mornings—and an open building to do the work in, something most U.S. adults and Christians expect from churches anyway. A strong majority of devoted Christians (70%) feels church buildings should be accessible all week).

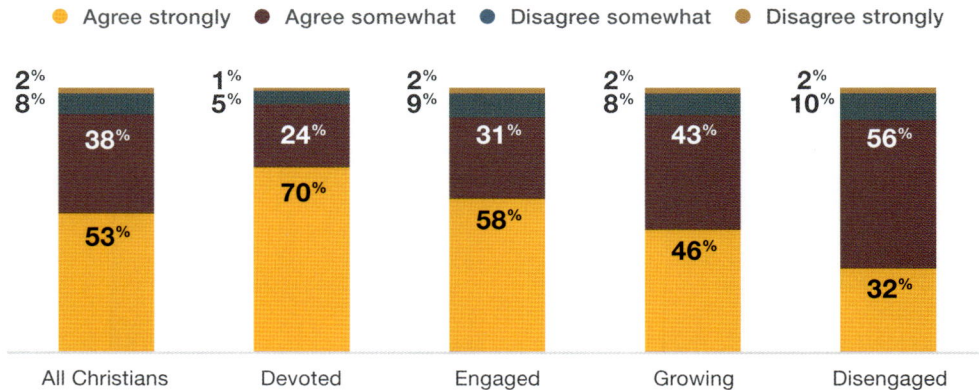

Keep in mind this comes with other responsibilities like staffing, security and upkeep. Such a

"Church Buildings Should be Accessible All Week"

● Agree strongly ● Agree somewhat ● Disagree somewhat ● Disagree strongly

	All Christians	Devoted	Engaged	Growing	Disengaged
Disagree strongly	2%	1%	2%	2%	2%
Disagree somewhat	8%	5%	9%	8%	10%
Agree somewhat	38%	24%	31%	43%	56%
Agree strongly	53%	70%	58%	46%	32%

n=1,238 U.S. adult Christians, February 28–March 9, 2022.

move should also be balanced with the expectation many people have for church buildings to "provide safety and security" (the survey did not specify whether this meant literal or figurative safety or security). About a third of all U.S. adults (31%) feel this is a role of the church. Christians who are not as far in their spiritual journey may especially look for safety and security. Two in five disengaged Christians (40%) say providing safety and security should be the purpose of a church's physical space.

Beyond serving the community, churches also have the unique opportunity to create beauty that can be enjoyed by anyone, free of charge—and this is a special way to celebrate the image of God in all people. Caring for others in this way can look like public art that contributes to the culture of the neighborhood, green spaces that exude peace and solace, or water features and wind chimes that pleasantly echo through the streets. Beauty in its various forms is a powerful way to share awe and inspiration with a church's community. (See page 44 for more thoughts on beauty and the church.) ●

Who's Connected?:
Welcome Neighbors Through Outreach & Ongoing Ministry

Meeting the physical needs of someone in crisis can empower them in many ways, including spiritually (just as serving others can be an important part of the spiritual formation of Christians). Those who have been cared for by your church may also want to participate in the worship and reflection spaces that your church space provides.

With this in mind, what might it look like for part of your building or church grounds to be more accessible to the public? Incorporating details to delight and surprise, including elements that have foot traffic and pedestrians in mind, is a way to be kind and loving to those in your community.

THE "PORTABLE" CHURCH: FOUR REMINDERS FOR MEANINGFUL GATHERING

Across the U.S., churches meet every Sunday in movie theaters, recreation centers, gymnasiums and other multipurpose spaces. Sometimes this is by choice, but often it's out of necessity. While these churches don't meet in a designated church building of their own, it doesn't mean their spaces can't operate with purpose. Here are some reminders to leaders following a portable church model:

Foster a sense of community: While a portable church may not have a permanent physical space, it's still possible to cultivate strong community. To do this, create a sense of ownership and involvement that extends beyond the needs for setup and breakdown. Plan social events and activities outside of regular services to help members connect and build relationships. Research nearby meeting spaces (or create your own) to encourage congregants to linger longer. There's also an opportunity to build relationships with other business owners, nonprofits and community entities through rental agreements and shared use.

Focus on meaningful worship experiences: Technology can be especially valuable to a portable church. While meeting in a gym may not exude the same transcendent experience as an actual church, lighting, backdrops and high-quality audio-visual equipment can help greatly. Make sure this equipment is well-placed and easy to set up, take down and transport.

Maximize storage and organization: Having dedicated storage space and an organized plan for setup and breakdown can help lessen the growing pains that come with being a mobile church. Even consider a practice run with your team and volunteers so they understand the full setup and breakdown process. Maybe you can rent a storage unit or a room at the venue where you meet to keep equipment nearby. As a bonus: Identify congregants who have a knack for organizing—or even a storage or organizing business of their own that you can support.

Remain flexible and adaptable: Portable churches have to embrace flexibility and adaptability. In turn, this brings opportunity for creativity. Encourage members to contribute their ideas for enhancing the worship experience and creating meaningful gatherings they want to invite friends and family to.

FROM THE ARCHITECT

At the end of each chapter, Derek DeGroot, president of Aspen Group and architect by trade, briefly shares helpful insight with the data in mind.

Jesus used countless examples from the material world as he taught his disciples. Their days were filled with sights of sheep, sowers, fishermen, the taste of bread and wine and so on. His teaching engaged the embodied world so that it was ever-present to the disciples even after he was physically gone.

If we're serious about discipleship, the life of our church should be no less embodied—and we can do this with the design of our church spaces. This doesn't mean everything important happens in your building, but it does mean that you should consider your church spaces as a critical place to show what it means to live every day as a disciple.

CASE STUDY

A NEW WAY OF SERVING

The respite of an oasis has long been welcomed by desert travelers, especially in arid regions like the Middle East and North Africa. They marked important stops along trade routes, providing water, food and a place of rest in otherwise dry, barren conditions. That's why the concept of an oasis is a common parallel in the Bible, figuratively depicting spiritual nourishment and God's miraculous provision. This poses the question: Are today's churches—or more specifically, is your church—viewed as an oasis … or a mirage?

Through the *Making Space* research, we learn there's a notable expectation (and desire!) that the church building be one that is helpful and useful to its community. Yet only 10 percent of Christians tell Barna that "providing resources for the community" is a top priority of their church. Certainly, most pastors would hope their church makes a difference in its community, meeting both spiritual and physical needs. So how can leaders ensure this goal doesn't get lost in the shuffle of other ministry responsibilities?

Bible Center Church, led by John Wallace Jr. and Cynthia Wallace, is one example of how incremental change can make a big difference. Through the church's community and economic development division, fittingly named The Oasis Project, they're revitalizing Pittsburgh's once-vibrant Homewood community (where Bible Center Church is located) by transforming vacant properties, creating public spaces and establishing third spaces for connection and collaboration.

"Our community looks visibly different because Bible Center is here," notes Cynthia, who serves as executive director of The Oasis Project. With this work, the church has built palpable trust with its neighbors and become the heartbeat of the community.

"This Building Is a Resource"

After moving back to Pittsburgh to lead Bible Center Church, which John's grandparents founded, the couple's ministry to the neighborhood started small—simply by picking up trash.

"We did this every Saturday for two years, [and] there was power in that because there was so much garbage," Cynthia recalls.

Residents took notice and began sharing their hearts with the pastors. In 2013, Bible Center officially launched The Oasis Project, which has evolved to include numerous outreach programs focused on the needs they heard from their neighbors, including a community kitchen, early learning center, business center, community garden and café.

"Churches are really central to communities. [They] should be that hub of community activity and community transformation," Cynthia says. "These are beautiful pieces of real estate that we need to maximize."

A key part of Bible Center's mission is adaptive reuse of abandoned and vacant properties. The church itself is a former drug store. Cynthia's office is in what was once an abandoned triplex. A shuttered post office is now the church's coffee shop. And an old grocery store is their business academy for underrepresented entrepreneurs.

"For all of our buildings, we have repurposed something. Bringing spaces back 'online' [is] advancing God's kingdom," Cynthia says.

She recommends these next steps for leaders asking the important questions concerning how their church can serve their community well:

1. **Get in tune with the gifts of current congregants.** "Each church is shaped differently," Cynthia reminds leaders. Because of this, it's important to understand the makeup of your church, rather than replicating what's done in other churches. "Who are the people that God has called to your ministry? What are their gifts? What are they bringing?" Answering these questions gives clarity to help them feel part of the bigger picture, both at church and in their community.

2. **Understand the felt needs of your neighbors.** To get a view of the needs and opportunities in your community, Cynthia recommends asset mapping. "When you're asset mapping, you're looking at what's there, what's missing and what's the need?" she explains. This means taking inventory of assets in the community—or the lack thereof. "Are there spaces that can be redeemed? Vacant buildings? Spaces that the church [can use] for something else?"

3. **Be open to partnership.** Much of the work Bible Center does is bolstered through partnership with organizations and individuals outside of their church. "[Community impact] doesn't mean the church acting independently," Cynthia explains. "It could be partnering with other organizations and institutions to say, "How can we make this community better?"

"All of what we have is in service to God. That's the heart change that happens initially. Then, [it's about] how we act that out. ... How do we use everything that we have for God's glory?"

THE CHURCH BUILDING: AN OFFERING TO THE BROADER COMMUNITY

Thoughts on the purpose of the church from Matthew Niermann, associate dean of the College of Architecture, Visual Arts & Design at California Baptist University

See page 10 to meet our contributors.

There is a phrase that pastors often use when considering building design: "We are not going to spend money on a building but are going to spend it on ministry and on the people of the community." While the heart behind this idea is well intentioned, my research shows that this is misguided. Consistently, in interview after interview and survey after survey exploring the unchurched perception of church buildings, churches that build a very plain, utilitarian, non-ecclesial building are viewed by the unchurched as not caring about their community and are perceived as selfish.

In a similar way, if a mayor decided that she wanted to build a library for a town and proposed to put up a shed-like building, the town would reject the plan and feel like the mayor did not have the best interest of the town in mind. Furthermore, even if the mayor said she was dramatically increasing library programing, this would do very little to change the initial perception. The library users may appreciate it, but most townspeople would prefer a beautiful building built as an enhancement to the town.

Architecture is fundamentally public and fundamentally contextual. Church buildings are seen as an offering to the broader community, particularly for nonusers, i.e., the unchurched. Thus, those congregations that build a building that is beautiful on the outside (not just the inside) are seen as a generous part of the community, and conversely, those congregations that build nonaesthetic, functionally driven buildings are viewed as selfish and not participating in the community.

Pastors should not overlook the fundamental idea that a building *does* communicate—particularly whether the building is in the public realm or a private institution. Our built environment is psychologically divided into four zones: public (anyone is welcome), semi-public (anyone is welcome, but you may be monitored), semi-private (you must have intention to go there) and private (only welcomed with invitation).

For example, in a typical residential scheme, the street and sidewalk are public, welcome to anyone without notice. The front lawn is semi-public such that people can step into the yard, but someone may give a look. The front porch is semi-private and requires intention to be on the porch. And finally, the house itself is private and requires an invitation to enter. These zones are built into our understanding of the built environment and apply to all buildings.

Unfortunately, our contemporary desire to make church attendees' lives easy by providing ample and visible parking has subtly worked against the public perception of the church.

Church buildings were traditionally sited on the front of the lot with doors open, effectively placing the church in the public / semi-public zone. However, when we locate the church in the back of the lot and place parking, landscaping and church signs between the sidewalk and the front door, we place the church in the private / semi-private zone.

I often hear pastors wonder why no one from the street walks in and uses their expensive café. The answer is found in the way the building communicates its relationship to the public realm. The church building visually and experientially communicates who God is and the centrality of worship, but we must also remember it communicates its publicness. ●

Q&A WITH
DUKE KWON

THE THEOLOGY OF PLACE

See page 10 to meet our contributors.

Q What is meant by a "theology of place," and why does it matter for today's Church?

A A theology of place is grounded, foremost, in a doctrine of creation; that God made us as physical human beings, both body and soul. Yet, we often ignore this to our detriment in our personal lives, our ecclesial lives and as church communities.

The Church, especially in this digital age, increasingly functions as though we can minister to people—both Christian and non-Christian—in fully disembodied ways. That's simply not the way the Bible describes who we are as human beings, and this is a theology that we urgently need to recover.

You often hear the phrase, "The church is the people, not a building." It's true that the Church is not, in its essence, a building, and that the body of Christ is, foremost, a people. But we also need to understand that, as embodied people, as physical people, our surroundings shape who we are and shape how we experience relationship and God himself.

Q In this research, we see that there is still an acknowledgment of the reverence of Christian churches today. What is your response to this as a pastor?

A There is a gradual movement away from the cultural centrality of the church in American life. Yet people still see the unique value of the presence of a church community at its best. The American public seems to still long for space that is set aside and set apart for the possibility of an encounter with God. People long for sacred space—not simply for a space that's relevant or a space that's accommodating, but a space where you can go and do the things you may not feel like you can do anywhere else: to meet with God or pray or move toward the transcendent. I'm encouraged that people would view the church as a place of safety, comfort and peace, even as, in other ways, the church has earned a reputation for being a place of threat, disruption and chaos. This shows there is still opportunity that we can capitalize on.

Q What advice would you give to leaders struggling to see the value in their church building, or who may be unsure how to start leveraging these physical spaces?

A There are pressing realities pastors are facing. It takes time to manage a building and all the leaky roofs and practical challenges that come along with it. This can inevitably raise the question, *Is it worth it? What is this physical space actually for?*

The starting point is not in the building itself, but rather in a clear understanding of the mission of the church. If we're clear on what we're trying to do and who we're trying to be, then the church building, as well as other tangible matters in church life, fit in as having strategic value to the mission of the church.

I believe that the church's mission is threefold: (1) worship of God, (2) nurture of the saints and (3) witness to our world. So I would raise questions like:

- Do we actually have spaces that enhance and support our worship?
- Are we creating a space for real encounters with our triune God? Is there true space for prayer?
- [Are we thinking about] people's sense of belonging? This involves the cultivation of relationships where people are supported through the trials and pains of life, and where people are formed, discipled and equipped to be servants of one another and our world.
- Do our buildings actually facilitate the formational process and the care process— bringing people together in community, training and equipping, and forming them into the likeness of Christ? ●

2

CONSIDER THE EXPERIENCE

Taste and see that the Lord is good.
Oh, the joys of those who take refuge in him!
— PSALM 34:8 (NLT)

"[Churches] have the capacity to gently mold within people a sense of the divine in both conscious and unconscious ways," Rev. Charles Chadwick, writing for the United Kingdom's National Churches Trust, reminds us. "They provide places for silence and calm, reflection and prayer.

"A beautiful and well cared for church can transmit something of the character of the Christian faith as well as the perception that this building is a place where God can be encountered," he continues. "In an age marked by distraction and uncertainty church buildings speak of permanence, stability and serenity. They can serve as places to withdraw to from the over-active and anxious times we live in."[10]

Intentional or not, church spaces actively shape and form the experience of those who occupy them. Next, we'll look at what these experiences might reveal about the spiritual formation happening inside a church building.

The Principle of Peace

In today's frenzied and frenetic world, peaceful experiences can be few and far between. A well-documented rise in anxiety—especially during and following the COVID-19 pandemic[11]—and increasing loneliness plague many adults today. Barna's report *Gen Z: Volume 2* indicates that younger generations in particular are struggling with widespread anxiety about important decisions and uncertainty about the future.[12] This need for peace begs for a place to experience it—and the church can be an answer.

Nearly half of all U.S. adults (47%) imagine they'd feel "peaceful" when sitting in a Christian church. Though we do see a significant dip in this number among younger generations (30% of Gen Z and 35% of Millennials), there is a general assumption that church will be a peaceful place, regardless of someone's spiritual beliefs.

We also know that, for those who are curious about God, there's a desire to experience peace in and through one's spirituality. In Barna's 2022 study *Spiritually Open*, peace and related themes like hope and healing are the top things spiritually open adults are looking for in their spiritual lives. Church spaces can be one way of inviting this; the experience of God's peace is a key component of the church experience, and a gateway to many other positive church experiences.

Engagement & Positive Emotions Rise Together

Spiritual formation is connected to positive emotions in church. Regardless of where a Christian is in their spiritual engagement, there are similarities in how believers imagine they might feel at church. Beyond peacefulness, Christians generally say they'd feel "connected to God" and "welcomed" in a Christian church.

The experience of these positive emotions deepens with spiritual engagement. Spiritual disengagement is accompanied by feeling less "valued" or "hopeful" in church. And just one in three

A Need for Peace

Imagine sitting in a Christian church.

Which of the following would you be most likely to feel?

(Top five answers of U.S. adults only)

● All U.S. adults ● Gen Z ● Millennials ● Gen X ● Boomers

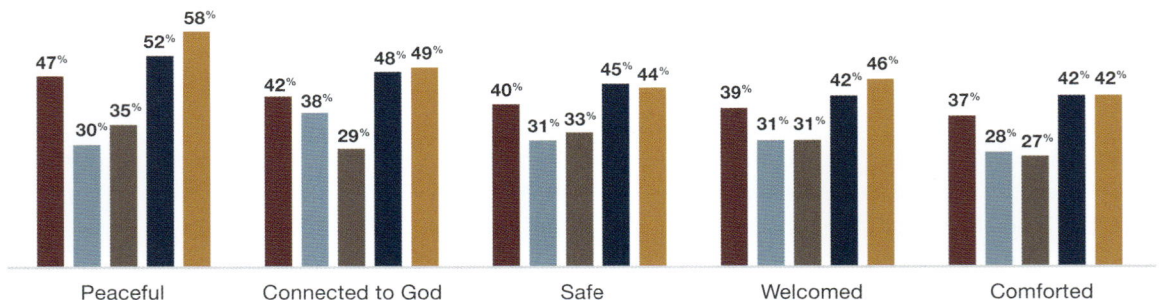

	Peaceful	Connected to God	Safe	Welcomed	Comforted
All U.S. adults	47%	42%	40%	39%	37%
Gen Z	30%	38%	31%	31%	28%
Millennials	35%	29%	33%	31%	27%
Gen X	52%	48%	45%	42%	42%
Boomers	58%	49%	44%	46%	42%

n=1,933 U.S. adults, February 28–March 9, 2022.

disengaged Christians (33%) says they would feel "connected to God" in a church, compared to more than double that among devoted Christians (70%). As a Christian moves from disengaged to growing, the expectation of a positive church experience greatly increases.

As Christians grow spiritually, their individual church experiences also improve and deepen. Three in four devoted Christians (77%) say they are "very satisfied" with their church (vs. 11% of disengaged Christians).

Perhaps this is because devoted Christians are more likely to be enmeshed in Christian community (61% say it is very true "I know many people at my church") and, therefore, may feel more deeply known. Feeling known is a fundamental human need defined as an individual's "ability to share their full life experiences, private thoughts and public image with important others."[13]

Church plays a more significant role in a devoted Christian's life now and into the future, giving them an assurance of community and stability as they age (three in four devoted Christians say it's very true "being part of my church is important to me" and "I expect to be part of my church for a long time").

Imagine sitting in a Christian church. Which of the following would you be most likely to feel?

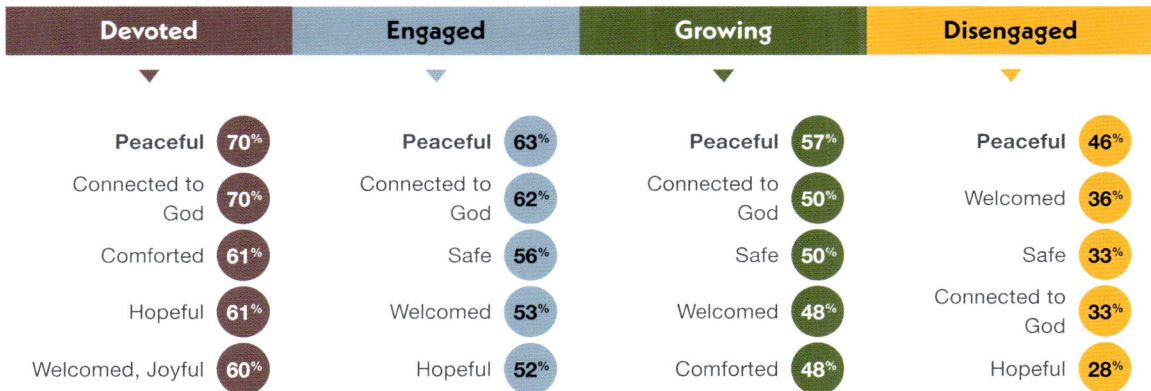

Devoted	Engaged	Growing	Disengaged
Peaceful **70%**	Peaceful **63%**	Peaceful **57%**	Peaceful **46%**
Connected to God **70%**	Connected to God **62%**	Connected to God **50%**	Welcomed **36%**
Comforted **61%**	Safe **56%**	Safe **50%**	Safe **33%**
Hopeful **61%**	Welcomed **53%**	Welcomed **48%**	Connected to God **33%**
Welcomed, Joyful **60%**	Hopeful **52%**	Comforted **48%**	Hopeful **28%**

n=1,238 U.S. adult Christians, February 28–March 9, 2022.

Devoted Christians Express High Satisfaction with Their Church

Still thinking about your church community, how true are the following statements?

Base: Christians

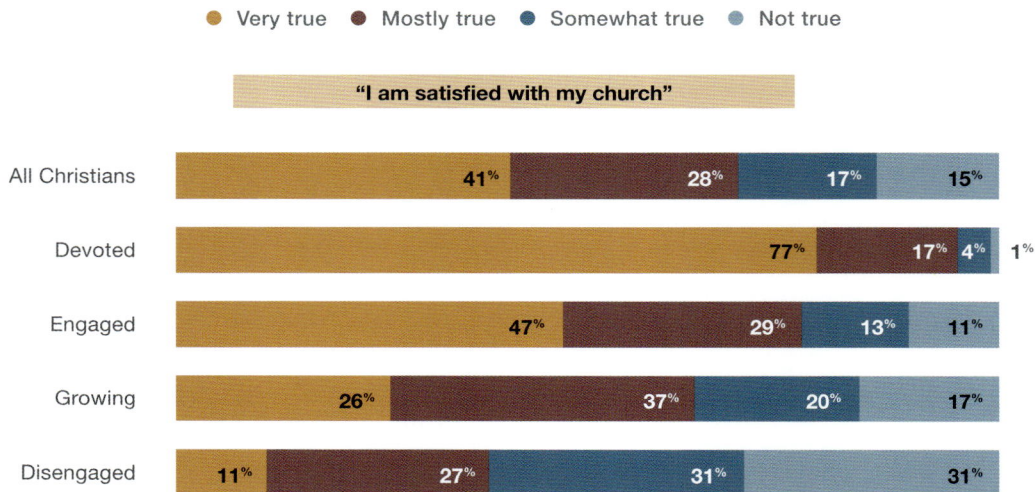

● Very true   ● Mostly true   ● Somewhat true   ● Not true

"I am satisfied with my church"

	Very true	Mostly true	Somewhat true	Not true
All Christians	41%	28%	17%	15%
Devoted	77%	17%	4%	1%
Engaged	47%	29%	13%	11%
Growing	26%	37%	20%	17%
Disengaged	11%	27%	31%	31%

n=1,238 U.S. adult Christians, February 28–March 9, 2022.

Who's Growing?: Elevate Spaces for Teaching, Learning & Discipleship

Spaces for preaching and instruction help congregants better understand the story of the gospel and its meaning in their life. The more engaged a Christian, the more likely they are to value sermons as an element of a meaningful church experience (77% of devoted Christians say preaching is "very important" vs. 30% of disengaged Christians). Spiritual formation births a desire to be filled with God's word, emphasizing the importance of a place for learning and growing.

Remember this data as you consider the environments where teaching and learning take place in your church: More than two-thirds of devoted Christians (70%) say their ideal church is "quiet." This number rises even higher—to 81 percent—for the disengaged. Most Christians (82%) also prefer a sanctuary over an auditorium. This doesn't mean large rooms aren't appropriate for Sunday mornings. It does, however, emphasize the significance of more intimate meeting spaces *somewhere* in your church.

With Spiritual Development Comes Deeper Connection to Faith Community

Thinking about your church community, how true are the following statements?

Base: Christians

● Very true   ● Mostly true   ● Somewhat true   ● Not true

"Being part of this church is important to me"

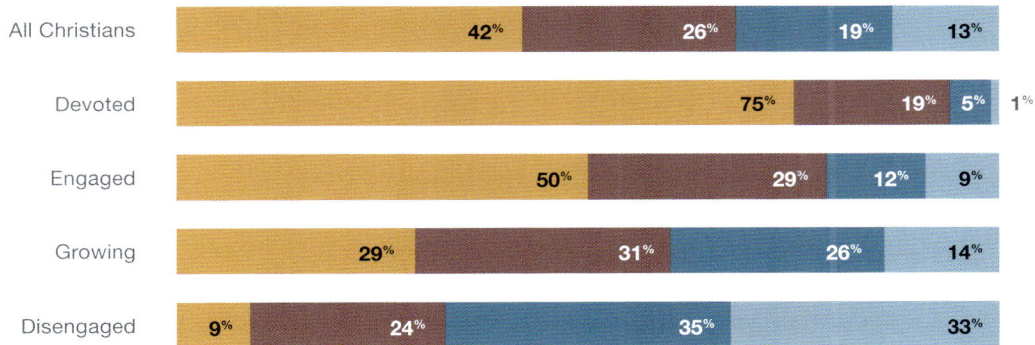

	Very true	Mostly true	Somewhat true	Not true
All Christians	42%	26%	19%	13%
Devoted	75%	19%	5%	1%
Engaged	50%	29%	12%	9%
Growing	29%	31%	26%	14%
Disengaged	9%	24%	35%	33%

"I expect to be part of my church for a long time"

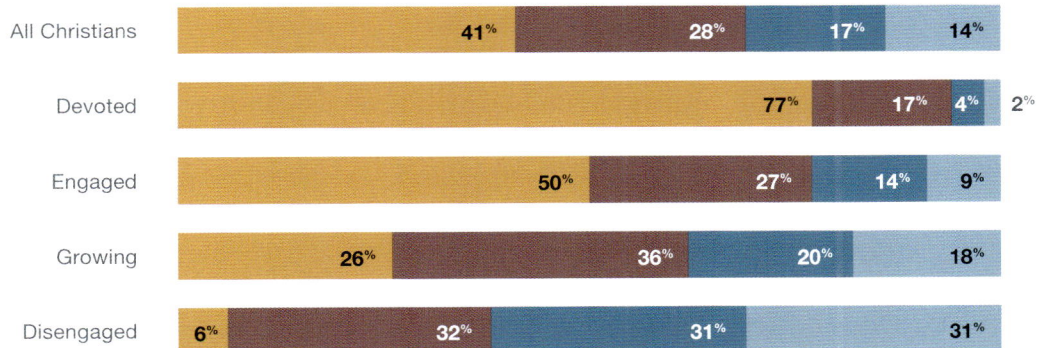

	Very true	Mostly true	Somewhat true	Not true
All Christians	41%	28%	17%	14%
Devoted	77%	17%	4%	2%
Engaged	50%	27%	14%	9%
Growing	26%	36%	20%	18%
Disengaged	6%	32%	31%	31%

n=1,238 U.S. adult Christians, February 28–March 9, 2022.

A Church Experience That Points to God

Above all else, Christians want to feel connected to God at church, and this desire increases with one's spiritual engagement. About half of disengaged Christians (48%) identify "connecting to God" as "very important" to a meaningful church experience, compared to nine in 10 devoted Christians (93%).

Engaged Christians also tend to be more emphatic about communal worship practices such as fellowship, praying together, reciting liturgy together and communion—all participatory aspects of church life. You may find those who are experiencing greater spiritual formation place a higher value on church design that reflects their valued experience of participation. Spaces that create room for engagement with others, such as breakout rooms, modular seating and even the layout of a sanctuary or main gathering space, can positively affect a Christian's church experience.

Service & Discipleship:
Two Key Areas Where Devoted Christians Stand Out

Which do you feel are the most important to having a meaningful experience at a Christian church?

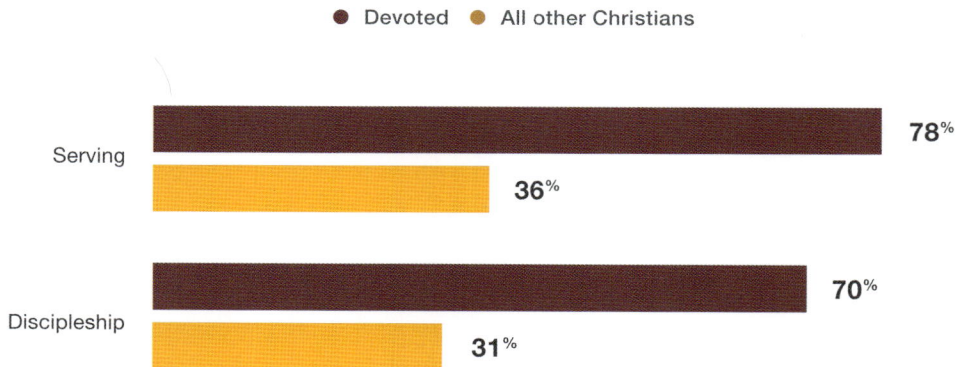

● Devoted   ● All other Christians

	Devoted	All other Christians
Serving	78%	36%
Discipleship	70%	31%

n=1,238 U.S. adults, February 28–March 9, 2022.

Church Design Can Help—or Hinder

It's important to remember that even Christians can experience confusion, uncertainty or discomfort at church. While some of these feelings decline as Christians move along the spectrum of spiritual engagement, nearly two in five growing Christians (36%) say, "I feel like there is a certain way I am supposed to behave at church." One in five growing Christians (22%) also admits, "Sometimes I feel uncomfortable in my own church." Both of these responses are higher than among disengaged Christians. Don't assume that more spiritually engaged congregants feel more at home at church or are having only positive church experiences. A Christian's faith walk can be varied, especially "in the middle" of the journey to confident devotion.

Growing Christians Need Space to Sort Through Uncertainties in Church

Are any of the following true of you?

Base: Christians

● Devoted   ● Engaged   ● Growing   ● Disengaged

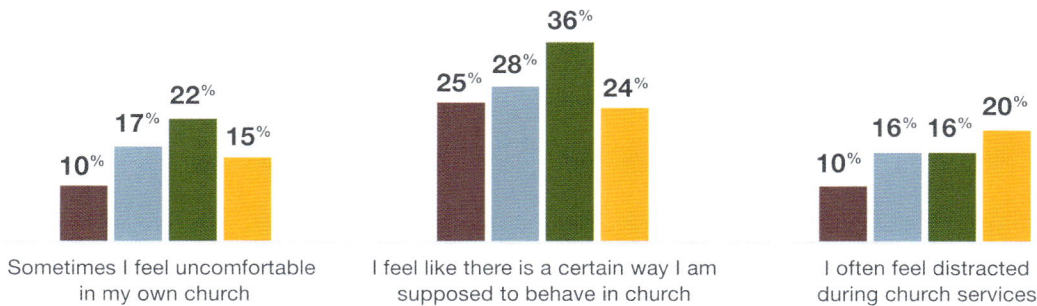

Sometimes I feel uncomfortable in my own church
- Devoted: 10%
- Engaged: 17%
- Growing: 22%
- Disengaged: 15%

I feel like there is a certain way I am supposed to behave in church
- Devoted: 25%
- Engaged: 28%
- Growing: 36%
- Disengaged: 24%

I often feel distracted during church services
- Devoted: 10%
- Engaged: 16%
- Growing: 16%
- Disengaged: 20%

n=1,238 U.S. adult Christians, February 28–March 9, 2022.

Who's Comfortable?: Don't Overlook Accessibility & Biblical Inclusivity

Comfort is about more than cushy seats, warm lighting and appropriate sound decibels; these are obvious design considerations. But have you thought about how the elderly or how those with mobility needs will use and navigate your space? What about the hearing impaired? (If this specific question feels daunting, start by adding captions to online videos.) Do people feel welcomed and included in your spaces? Comfort and hospitality are about creating an environment where people can focus on connecting with God and others without added concerns about what is expected or required. It's a place where they can feel at ease, seen and valued.

Creating spaces that address some of the discomforts people can experience at church is a meaningful way to communicate "you are welcome here." Incorporate spaces for people to "duck out" of the social interactions or pressures if certain activities are overwhelming at first. Help them make the emotional adjustments necessary to stick it out through discomfort. This might look like

- Putting a sofa on the edge of a busy room for people to find a moment of respite.
- Creating a quiet room or chapel where the architecture encourages silence and reflection. This allows people to participate in a less intense way.
- Creating solitary spaces within a busy room, like a small pedestal table with paper and pens for people to be "alone in the crowd" for a moment.

Some uncertainty can be greatly diminished with a little foresight by church leaders. Helping people feel cared for means thinking about them *before* they enter the building.

While the conflict of how to behave in church will always be present, assess how your church can help remove or lessen anxious thoughts and concerns. You can almost guarantee a visitor will have questions they may not feel comfortable asking: *Where should my children go? Do I read this Psalm out loud? Should I stand? Sit? Where is the closest bathroom?* ●

Make sure there is directional signage that is easy to understand. You don't want visitors to feel like your church is a secret club where everyone knows where to go except them. Ensure the restrooms, main entrance, sanctuary and kids' ministry spaces are easily identified. If people feel like they don't fit in or can't find their way around on their own, they may not return.

Also, if you'd like to know how visitors perceive your space, invite a visitor to come as a "secret shopper" to your church. After their visit, ask them to share their experience with you. Ask them how inviting your space was and if it was easy to navigate and find things. You may be surprised by their answers. Use their input to guide your future designs.

—Heather Sibinksi

ELEMENTS OF
A WELCOMING SPACE

Welcome has two sides: Extending vulnerability and helping someone feel safe to do the same. Here are some ways you can do this through your spaces:

Vulnerability requires sharing a bit of ourselves. Don't be afraid to be personal in your church space. "Brand storytelling" and personal expression are practices that help people understand who and what a church is about. Amplify the real people who live in your church; help people see what happens there.

Consider ways to provide psychological safety and comfort. For people unfamiliar with your church, knowing where to go is a great place to start. But also give them something to do! That's why coffee is about more than the coffee itself—it's a way to participate.

Give people opportunity to engage in a low-stakes way. For example, put analog games on tables or create a focal point or something to browse, offering a conversational opening. The overall design of a space can help elements like this make intuitive sense, and when a space feels congruent, it can add to the psychological comfort people experience. Welcoming spaces take into consideration what happens between not knowing someone and making introductions. These spaces give people a chance to explore and engage without being so vulnerable that it's uncomfortable.

One churchgoer in a Barna-led focus group for the *Making Space* project described a safe and comfortable space like this: "There's just something about getting coffee or food with other people and sitting in that little room. Even if you're not talking to anyone else … you'll be around other people. You don't really have to talk about religion or anything. It just seems like anyone could walk in and have something to eat or drink and sit down. There's nothing really barring anyone from [participating]."

FROM THE ARCHITECT

At the end of each chapter, Derek DeGroot,
president of Aspen Group and architect by trade,
briefly shares helpful insight with the data in mind.

We had some striking conversations in this research process around what a peaceful space feels like. It was almost counterintuitive when people referred to a cavernous cathedral with soaring ceilings and massive stained glass windows as a place that felt peaceful because it made them "feel small."

I think one of the gifts a church is able to give people is a space where they don't always have to be in charge. Ten years ago, we talked about how Millennials wanted modularity, the ability to change and choose their own experience. But now people are stressed, overwhelmed by the options, and there's actually a sense of peace that comes from feeling like they are not responsible for the world. They are small, and they have a big Creator. Their future and security is in his hands.

Few churches can swap out their sanctuary for a cathedral, but you can bring in elements that remind people of a big God who loves them. Experiment with window openings and natural light. Install a piece of art that invites people to look up. Maybe even reduce decision fatigue by creating clear visual expectations for what's done in the space. For example, instead of immediately directing visitors to an information booth, offer a small garden walk where the only thing a person is asked to do is put one foot in front of the other.

HARMONY & PROPORTION: UNDERSTANDING THE INGREDIENTS OF A BEAUTIFUL CHURCH

Thoughts on beauty and the church from David Taylor, author and associate professor of theology & culture at Fuller Theological Seminary

See page 10 to meet our contributors.

What is it about the concept of beauty that helps us describe the world as it ought to be? It comes down to two things: Harmony, or symmetry, and proportion.

Let me give you an example from something that I do. I make salsas. One is a habanero salsa. Proportionally, it has one white onion, three tomatoes chopped kind of chunky, two habaneros and a little bit of avocado or olive oil in a pan, and then you sauté everything. Then you put the ingredients in a blender, add two tablespoons of apple cider vinegar, blend it up, put it back in the pan and simmer until it really cooks into the deliciousness you want. Harmony happens as all the parts work together and come together to make a salsa that I've made over the years. My family loves it, and every time we eat it we're like, "This is amazing." Because I've figured out the recipe.

Now, some people may not like their salsa as hot as we like it, so they might use one habanero rather than two. Some people might like their salsa slightly sweeter, so they'll add more tomatoes. That's the question of proportion: How do all the ingredients come together? And symmetry is how they all hold together.

If I put in 20 tomatoes, it's going to make the flavor really weird. The sweetness and acidity of the tomato turns the salsa all wrong. If I put 10

habaneros in, it scorches your mouth, and there's nothing pleasant about that.

Such experiences are what I call "ugly." The proportion is all wrong, and how the ingredients hold together is all wrong. When something is beautiful, each individual part is right, and what each part does together is right. They come together and create an experience of *wholeness*.

Every time we experience something beautiful, what we're actually experiencing is a taste of the entirety of the *shalom* of God. Right now, we can only taste it in part. And every experience of beauty is an anticipation of a world where everything is as it should be, according to God.

Christian leaders and organizations often ask, "What does beauty look like? What does it mean? How do we measure whether we are doing things that are beautiful or not?"

Here is what we must consider:

1. **What are we (the Church) making?** What are we putting out into the world? Does it evoke wonder in God's creation? Does it cause people to look around and marvel? The fact that this world has over 7,000 kinds of apples, far exceeding any biological or spiritual necessity—what does that say about God? What does it say about the character of God, the works of God and what God requires of us to enter into the never-ending wonderment of the world?

2. **Does it cause people to experience the infinite desirability of God?** We've probably accomplished effective, productive things in the name of God, for the sake of the mission of God. But does the result of what we've done cause people to desire God, to yearn for him?

3. **Does it generate in us a yearning to be more like Jesus?** If, through what we make, we aren't able to cause one another to be more like Jesus, and to perceive others with the dignity and beauty of the image of God in them no matter how dastardly and pernicious they may be in actual practice, then maybe we're failing to do the work that beauty requires of us.

4. **Have we utilized those who can make our work more beautiful?** Are artists and designers at the table—those who have a keen, acute intuition and skill for the aesthetic dimension? Artists and creatives help us understand why our senses and bodies play such an important role in how we exist in the world, perceive ourselves and do the work of the Kingdom. ●

Q&A WITH
MICHAEL SCHEER

FORMATION & THE ARTS

See page 10 to meet our contributors.

Q What should church leaders understand about ecclesiastical art and its significance to the spiritual formation of congregants?

A Historically, we've always had art in the church, and the primary goal of this was to teach. Stained glass was first used because churches needed a way to get across the messages and stories of the Bible to people who were illiterate.

Today, we live in a heavily visual culture. When you have a lot of people who are constantly inundated with visuals online, and living in a culture of visual learning, we should embrace that and say, "Let's go back to our roots and get some of that education back in the church in an artistic way."

Q Why should church leaders care about beauty in their church? What does a beautiful church communicate?

A Churches have such a responsibility to provide help, support, care and community. Sometimes, we get the idea that we [can't] do those things and have enough funds left over to do the artistic things. While art typically costs money—it's not a cheap thing to do, especially when you're using fine materials—scripture tells us to offer our best to God. Ask, what *can* we do, even if we don't have a huge budget?

Our congregations are people. That's where a lot of those resources lay. There are probably artistic people in every church. How can we tap into those resources that are already in the church?

Q Our data shows that most Christians agree, "Church buildings should reflect the beauty of God." But just 37 percent of Christians say, "I believe my church building is beautiful." What are some practical steps to bridging this gap?

A Do a Q&A with your congregation, form a committee and create visual statements about your church. This can be as simple as asking: *Do we believe the church building to be the house of God, or the house of God's people? Is it both? Is it one or the other? Is it neither?* When we answer questions like this, we start to coalesce an understanding and galvanize the whole picture that we can see about our beliefs in the church.

Then, you can get into the process of asking: *How are we expressing these beliefs visually? If we're not expressing them, how can we bring that in? If we are expressing something visually that isn't in alignment with these beliefs, how can we change that?*

[This can then inform] the visual decisions a church is making. *Do we want fake flowers, or do we want real flowers? What does it say to have something that is fake versus something that's authentic and growing?*

Often, churches are hesitant to jump into aesthetics because there are disagreements in the church about aesthetics. You might have someone who likes a very modern aesthetic. You might have someone who likes a very traditional aesthetic. [Visual statements] can curb those disagreements by allowing common ground that we can talk about.

Q

Can you share a story or experience where you partnered with a church or Christian organization to provide custom artwork? How was it mutually beneficial?

A We did a project with a child and family services organization to help with their chapel [that was also] a multipurpose space. They wanted stained glass windows that would help teach Bible stories to kids they served who might not have much of an understanding or much experience with the church.

We worked with an illustrator who does children's book illustrations, because we wanted a very illustrative look that could help these kids understand the different stories in scripture that are important to their faith formation. Now, whenever they use this space, whether it's for assemblies, for chapel services or other gatherings for these kids, they have this object to look at.

This was an opportunity to take a blank canvas and ask: *What can we do here that can support and help the people that are in this space the most?"*

That was a very fruitful project for us and for them because it allowed us to partner with an illustrator who didn't have a lot of opportunity to do that kind of work but was very excited about it, and also partner with the organization and provide something that really supported their mission and what they were doing in a beautiful and aesthetically pleasing way. ●

CASE STUDY

A NEW WAY OF ENGAGING

Throughout this *Making Space* series, we've challenged leaders to think of ways their existing church spaces can be used in different, more purposeful ways—especially if budget is not yet sufficient for a new build or larger renovation. *How can you make the most of what you already have?*

One often overlooked asset is the land a church sits on—or for Christ Lutheran Church in Charlotte, North Carolina, the land across the street. Since its inception in 2018, the church's Growing to Give garden ministry has produced over 5,700 pounds of fresh vegetables, most of which is donated to area food pantries and other community partners. Co-managers Walt Roth and David Deeds have seen firsthand how the growth from this space, both literal and figurative, has drawn people closer to God, church and community.

God-Sized Provision

In April 2016, a neighbor across the street from Christ Lutheran's South Charlotte campus approached leaders about the sale of her lot, for which the congregation made an offer. According to Deeds, funds were raised in three weeks to pay for the property. After acquiring the one-acre lot, the church decided to tear down an outdated home on the land.

The heart behind the garden ministry is one of complete thankfulness for what our Lord continues to grace us with out of pure divine love. [It allows us to] demonstrate our faith so that others see what is unique about our Lord and Savior, Roth adds. Our corner garden sign is welcoming all to "Come Grow With Us" and that alone has some people stopping by when they see us working the garden.

—Walt Roth

"That God-sized hole was filled with dirt that 'just so happened' to have been excavated from a sewer project less than a mile from Christ Lutheran," Deeds recalls. "The contractor gifted 100 truckloads of dirt and the related grading (valued at $43,000) to the church."

Inspired by the community garden at his daughter's church in North Raleigh, Roth proposed starting a garden on what was now fertile ground.

Before it was even official, the garden ministry team quickly grew to more than 20 members—all pitching in to make Growing to Give a success. In its first year, the garden raised 628 pounds of fresh vegetables that were donated to a local food bank. The next year, that crop tripled and has continued to increase each year thereafter.

Planting a community garden at your church could be a multifaceted way to change lives in your congregation and community. Here's some of what Christ Lutheran has experienced:

1. **Deeper commitment to church mission:** With each effort to fund and run the garden, Christ Lutheran saw more congregants band together in inspiring ways. Many of the garden beds were built by the hands of church members. Whether giving, building, teaching, planting, watering or harvesting, the garden has expanded each season with more gardeners and volunteers, and thus more fresh produce (and knowledge) to share.

2. **Expanded community and social connection:** A community garden serves as a unique gathering place where there's shared purpose and wide-open space to enjoy nature and each other. "Christian community was formed among the gardeners who [were simply] following Jesus' command to love our neighbors," Deeds says, adding that the gardeners have often united to "work together, build camaraderie, make new friends, enjoy God's great outdoors and continue to pray and give Jesus thanks."

3. **Fulfillment of community needs:** More than 95 percent of the produce Christ Lutheran harvests is shared with neighbors in need. The garden's impact was especially notable during the pandemic. While previous years' harvests benefited local food pantries, 2020's harvest of nearly 2,700 pounds of produce was shared with families in need from the nearby middle school. The ministry has also helped families in its congregation, including gardeners. "It's an opportunity for me to love my neighbors practically," Deeds says. "[But] a garden ministry is not just about producing food; it's about cultivating the soul, deepening one's faith and glorifying God through stewardship and service."

4. **Opportunities for intergenerational relationships:** In Growing to Give's first year, local Boy Scouts and their families got involved as a way to achieve Eagle Scout rank. "They constructed raised beds, laid pavers for a garden entrance work area, added a

> The garden ministry has helped build relationships, compassion and a sense of belonging among us gardeners. It is another opportunity for me to love my neighbors. Planting seeds and watching them grow with patience is like my interactions with people that the Holy Spirit has placed in my life who are seeking Jesus.
>
> **—David Deeds**

harvesting table and built a table and benches so folks could sit and enjoy God's creation in the garden," Deeds explains.

Additionally, "Several gardening families have brought their young children to help, giving them knowledge and understanding of where at least some of their food comes from—God's earth, not a grocery store."

5. **Flourishing people and a thriving church:** Purchasing that acre of land proved to be beneficial not only for congregants and the surrounding community. In 2021, as Charlotte's real estate market boomed, Christ Lutheran decided to sell the property, which had at least tripled in value in just a few years.

With this profit, the garden ministry was moved and expanded to Christ Lutheran's other two campuses. Proceeds were also designated as seed money for the construction of a multi-use worship space and other outreach efforts. ●

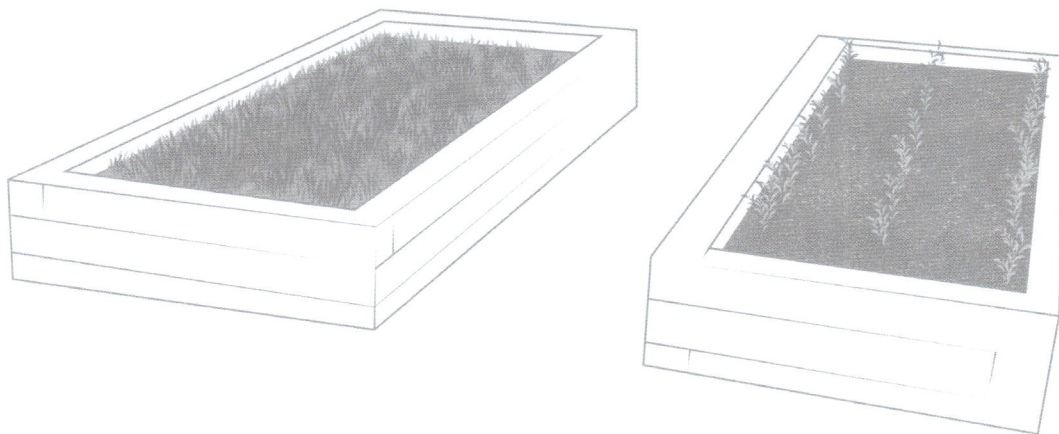

WHEN SPACE DISCIPLES

Barna grouped Christians to focus on those who are most rooted in a church community—and, inevitably, spend more time in church buildings and spaces. Through this lens, we see anew that:

- Proximity to the life of the local church is a boost to spiritual formation.
- Christians with slight church connections are often in a lukewarm season of discipleship.
- Distance from a local church correlates with a lack of belonging and low desire for the things of God.

This infographic zooms in on these segments and highlights the importance of creating and being in meaningful church spaces.

Rooted	Involved	Intrigued	Distant

Rooted Christians are very connected to their church. They have church community and strongly agree "I engage with my church in more ways than just attending worship services" and "being part of this church is important to me."

Intrigued Christians have church community but tend to hang out on the sidelines. They may be curious about the church experience but disagree "I engage with my church in more ways than just attending worship services" or "being part of this church is important to me."

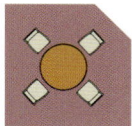

Involved Christians have church community but participate in the church experience to a lesser degree. They somewhat agree "I engage with my church in more ways than just attending worship services and "being part of this church is important to me."

Distant Christians are overall disconnected from the churchgoing experience. They do not view themselves as part of a church community.

Rooted ● Involved ● Intrigued ● Distant

What's "very important" to a meaningful church experience?

Greater Yearning for God

When an individual is connected to their church, formational practices are essential to their experience of that sacred space.

Presence of the Holy Spirit
● 91% ● 53% ● 68% ● 55%

Learning about the Bible
● 90% ● 55% ● 55% ● 41%

Growing closer to Jesus
● 90% ● 60% ● 66% ● 56%

Praying together
● 87% ● 57% ● 55% ● 43%

Worshipping together
● 86% ● 42% ● 55% ● 40%

High Discipleship Engagement

Three in four rooted Christians are being discipled and feel a deep responsibility to share their faith with others.

Who's currently being discipled

● 76% ● 56% ● 41% ● 22%

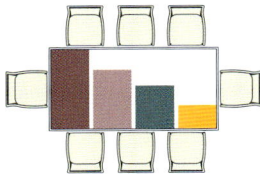

"I have a personal responsibility to tell other people about my religious beliefs."
% strongly agree

75% 20% 20% 18%

Lasting Commitment to the Church Body

Rooted Christians have a heightened sense of fulfillment and satisfaction with their church and are typically in it for the long run.

% say "very true"

My church helps me grow spiritually
● 90% ● 35% ● 34% ● 20%

I expect to be part of my church for a long time
● 90% ● 26% ● 31% ● 16%

I feel comfortable in my church
● 89% ● 37% ● 37% ● 21%

I am satisfied with my church
● 87% ● 25% ● 33% ● 17%

n=1,238 U.S. adult Christians, February 28–March 9, 2022.

3

PLAN WHAT'S NEXT

Let us think of ways to motivate one another to acts of love and good works. And let us not neglect our meeting together, as some people do, but encourage one another, especially now that the day of his return is drawing near.

—HEBREWS 10:24-25 (NLT)

Around the 150th anniversary of the founding of his parish, priest and theologian John Stott wrote this about the purpose of the church:

> We are not only Christian people; we are also church people. We are not only committed to Christ; we are also committed to the body of Christ. ... For the church lies at the very center of the eternal purpose of God. It is not a divine afterthought. It is not an accident of history. On the contrary, the church is God's new community. For his purpose, conceived in a past eternity, being worked out in history and to be perfected in a future eternity. It is not just to save isolated individuals and so perpetuate our loneliness, but rather to build his church, that is, to call out of the world a people for his own glory.[14]

This sort of calling for the church—as a people and as a place—deserves careful thought, vision, planning and action. Too often church members and visitors aren't clear on the vision of the church they are attending. And even if they are, there can still be a disconnect between that vision and how it is represented in the church building.

In the data, we get a glimpse of how spiritual engagement and church vision may be connected. One in five disengaged Christians (22%) are not sure what their church's highest priority is (vs. just 1% of devoted Christians, 6% engaged, 7% growing).

Generally, people want to attend a church that is familiar—a place where they know what to expect—and consistent—a place they can trust and count on.

With all of this in mind, it's appropriate to end this journal with questions and tools that will help you manifest your church's vision through the use of your church's space. In this chapter you'll find tips and recommendations for key spaces in any church.

Your Outdoor Spaces

A church's outreach ultimately welcomes people into a transcendent place where they can experience Christ. Knowing that most people associate nature and a sense of peace and calm with transcendent, spiritual spaces, it may be time to plan an outdoor space.

Design Elements to Consider

- Connect your church's outdoor spaces to the community. For example, create sidewalks that flow into other public areas or nearby neighborhoods. This makes it easier for pedestrians to access your space.

- Does your church have a garden? Remember to tend to this space through the seasons. Mix up what's planted for spring, summer, fall and winter. A good garden requires maintenance, but is an inexpensive way to create visual interest, variety and beauty for people to enjoy.
- Incorporate signs or directions along a pathway like a prayer walk. Invite people to pray at various stations or share scriptures that connect people to nature and their creator, like Psalm 19 or Psalm 24.

Your Parking Lot & Lobby

A welcoming church is one that strives to create an atmosphere where visitors feel valued, accepted and included. From making those unfamiliar with church feel comfortable to removing perceived barriers to participation—when done well, this intentionality conveys the message "you belong here."

The parking lot and lobby are often the first impression visitors have of a church, so its design should prioritize creating a welcoming, informative and accessible environment that reflects the church's values and mission.

Design Elements to Consider

- Curb appeal is important even for a church. Yet, nowadays, parking lots often take up a significant portion of the land a church sits on. Where possible, plan green spaces that break up concrete and pavement. Don't underestimate the power of simply planting trees. If your building sits far back from the road, what can you bring closer to the curb to help people get excited about what's going on inside? Changing an exterior façade or adding curb appeal are simple ways to show the community

Gardens around religious spaces are places of community connection and personal introspection. Moments with nature allow us to connect with living things large and small and find our place in an ever-changing fabric that is greater than ourselves. These experiences have the power to restore and nourish us on our spiritual journey.

—Ryan Moody

that your church is invested in and cares about the neighborhood—including how neighbors enjoy the building's exterior.

- Use shared spaces to connect your property with the rest of the community. Consider a pocket park, dog park, splash pad, playground or other amenity the community can enjoy. This communicates to every passer-by that your church is alive and available for them.
- Upon entering your church, make sure people are met with a positive experience and know how to navigate your space. A designated hospitality and / or greeting area to welcome and assist visitors can create a warm and friendly atmosphere. Visible signage and clarity (see "wayfinding" on page 13) are essential. Ensure visitors of all ages and capabilities can comfortably get around and know where to go.
- Place different seating styles in different areas of your lobby. A mixture of soft seating, stools and standing tables, for instance, can help people naturally assess your space for opportunities to connect.
- Try putting places to sit on the edges of the main flow of your lobby to allow people a full vantage point of what's happening in the room. You can highlight these peripheral areas through slight changes in design like different flooring, seating or a ceiling feature.

Your Children's Spaces

Children's ministry impacts the heart of your church now and in the future. Barna's 2022 report *Children's Ministry in a New Reality* tells us that children who have a meaningful relationship with an adult in the church are more likely to be rooted in scripture, Children's ministry and the life of the church and to externalize their faith. Youth ministry is a powerful opportunity to form lasting faith in the lives of young people—and in your church.

Yet data from that study also revealed a majority of children's ministry leaders feel children's ministry is often forgotten by their church (even as pastors, parents and congregants say children's ministry should be a priority).

Caring for the youth in your church will require *visible* action. And a great way to do this is in the design of your spaces.

[With youth space], you get to make it fun! Think through the lens of kids and youth. What do they enjoy? What can you add to the space to make them want to be there? Get input from the leaders over those areas. They know best how they will use the space and what the youth like.

In our kids and youth spaces, we use bright colors and trending designs but pull in repeating design cues and accents throughout the building to keep a unified look.

—Heather Sibinski

Design Elements to Consider

- Good design is always managing tension. One such tension is that great kids and youth spaces are an opportunity for intergenerational spaces where adults want to be, too. But the intergenerational strength becomes a challenge in terms of parent expectations for safety.

- When managing that tension to design youth spaces where adults also want to be, start with your kids' environment and don't overdo the theming. Colors don't have to be fluorescent, and you can incorporate opportunities to delight and surprise (like a round window, a staircase to something special, a storytelling element, or a light that has a different color). Keep it connected to the adult spaces, too, helping kids know that one day they'll be "out there" in the sanctuary. As they get older, envision their future as adult Christians by allowing them to participate in the adult spaces.

- For great intergenerational space, create play spaces in your public domains where adults also connect! This provides opportunities for kids to engage close to the adults, allowing parents to keep an eye on the kids, but also allowing the kids to interact with the adults.

- Don't always overstimulate—help kids practice prayer and quiet, too. Create comfortable and calm spaces for elementary school and older children to start engaging these spiritual disciplines, too. Create spaces for them to explore with artifacts and textures, engaging all their senses in a learning experience.

Your Gathering Spaces

Making space for fellowship and community reminds people they aren't alone in their spiritual journey. This is especially important at a time when over half of U.S. adult Christians (56%) say their spiritual life is "entirely private."[15] Christians who share this sentiment are also less likely to say their faith is very important in their life today, or to have weekly time with God.[16] Regularly attending a small group or Bible study also isn't a common practice among Christians today.

Devoted Christians do report practicing these spiritual rhythms at a higher rate. And, as noted in chapter 2, this group is more likely to value the communal aspects of Christianity.

Design Elements to Consider

- Help people linger. Give them something to do, provide food and drink, give them seating options.

- Open up the building for small groups and Bible studies. You'd probably be surprised that many churches don't let small groups use the building for weeknight groups. How can you be creative with security to allow people to host small groups in the building if they don't have enough space in their homes?

- How can you connect the building more to the neighborhood, whether that includes residential areas or businesses? The spiritual lives of Christians aren't wholly private, and the church doesn't need to be isolated from the community, either. Invite people onto the property, structurally and in more formal ways, like making the parking lot available for local kids to play basketball. ●

There's a lack of third spaces in our culture. There are not a lot of opportunities to [encounter] spaces where people can get together [outside of a workplace or home], and feel connected. Churches are that place. But it's hard when a church might not feel like a welcoming space [to others]—even if it works for your congregation.

If you have a beautiful space, people want to spend time there. We see this with the entire field of interior design, ranging from hotels to office buildings; people want to be in nice spaces. If [the Church] can provide a space for people to worship where they want to be and want to come back to, even for reasons outside of the worship aspect, we're setting ourselves up for success.

—**Michael Scheer**

THE CHURCH ON A BUDGET:
FIVE LOW-COST WAYS TO RENEW YOUR SPACES

Veteran church interior designer Rachel Reed knows firsthand the nuances that come with new builds and renovations.

"As a pastor's wife, I have not only been part of replanting a church but have taken on an intense building program of our own. I have seen the ups and downs and all the financial burdens that come with church growth. I have felt the spiritual and physical exhaustion it takes, and just when I thought I had it all together, God would bring me back to my knees.

"Our building program was one of those 'faith seasons,' filled with unexpected turns and a roller coaster of emotions. It was a learning curve, and I know it is for so many that call ministry their true calling."

Here are her tips for achieving small design victories that make a big difference:

Clean the building
Wash the walls, mop the floors, weed the garden beds and dust off the cobwebs in the corners. This is really the first step to a more welcoming church.

Declutter
Churches can be hoarding grounds. They hold on to every decoration, craft supply or church record, and it all piles up and spills out everywhere.

A good rule of thumb: If you haven't used it in this last year, throw it away, donate it or sell it. Go paperless (where it makes sense) and get reputable church management software to stay organized. Learn to love a minimal church. Keep it simple. Keep it focused.

Use your congregants' skills
See if there are people in your church with specific skill sets for renovation. Give them a clear plan of what you want with a sketch or a designer's rendering. Always offer to pay individuals, but you may find that some will choose to give their time as an act of generosity to the church.

Start with one project
Focus on one project, done excellently. This not only creates excitement among congregants for future projects, but it will also show guests that your church is alive and ready for them—and whatever the future may bring.

Seek out grants or donations
Many companies will give building supplies, paint, even playground equipment or furniture to nonprofit organizations. It may take time to organize, but gifts like this can help serve your church by reducing the costs of renovating.

See page 72 for more on church design budgeting.

FROM THE ARCHITECT

At the end of each chapter, Derek DeGroot,
president of Aspen Group and architect by trade,
briefly shares helpful insight with the data in mind.

People who study human behavior found out a long time ago that if you change an environment, you change the way people act. And if you change the way people act, you eventually change the way they think. As my colleagues and I design and build spaces for churches, we're working from the conviction that your church building is actually a high-leverage opportunity to disciple your congregation. Your church spaces currently speak a language (a building language, so to speak) that is not neutral. It is either working in alignment with your stated culture or actively working against it.

You will navigate many competing priorities in a building project. Having trustworthy partners who understand the mission of your church will be critical to the discernment process. The metrics of success will be nonlinear, much like a discipleship journey. But here are a few tips to help you get started:

- Have people from outside your church tour the space and ask them what your church values, based on what they see in the building.
- Host a town hall and discuss what memories different spaces bring up in people. Spaces represent functional needs and emotional needs.
- Start with temporary changes. What happens when you close a side entry door or move where the coffee is? What if you change the seating arrangement or add art? What changes in behaviors can you document and reflect on?
- What happens differently when you have the same function in a new space? Does an outdoor classroom provoke different responses than an indoor one?

Q&A WITH
JESSICA GRACEWSKI

SPACE FOR CHURCH MISSION

See page 10 to meet our contributors.

Q The mission of Reality San Francisco is "a community following Jesus, seeking renewal in our city." What does renewal look like in your context, and how is your church uniquely equipped to respond to this need?

A Just like the diversity of our city and context, we hope renewal is shaped and determined by the people of God—to be with Jesus, to become like Jesus and to do what he did. Renewal is the goal of how we, both individually and collectively, are able to [be] directed and guided by God.

We hope that our space and the places we find ourselves in can bring about this journey of becoming more like Jesus. As we [share the use] of our space with our community, congregants and others, [this become a place] to practice being with God (presence) and with others (participation), not to mention, it supports our values of generosity and hospitality.

Q In our research, we see a significant desire for safety and comfort in the church experience. Thinking about today's culture and society, why do you think this is? What's needed for the church to be a place where people can feel safe and like they belong?

A One of the most beautiful things church was created for is to embody what it means to *belong*. At the core of the fears about safety or discomfort is the bigger desire for a sense of belonging. I often experience discomfort when I am fearful I may not "fit in," or I really desire to belong but am scared others might reject me.

The physical space of a church is one that can be developed in imaginative ways to [help others] express and embody belonging.

Q Presence and participation are two key practices your church endeavors to uphold. How is this lived out in the physical spaces of your church and beyond?

A Presence and participation are part of our discipleship as Christ followers. It accounts for how we are present to one another and to God, as well as how we participate and partner with God and others. How we embody this and who we invite into our space reflects aspects of God—not just for the sake of the individuals we are serving, but how we, as followers of God, give and receive what we have in Christ and how Christ is expressed to those in our surrounding area.

Q Your church building is unique in both its structure and location. How have these physical characteristics helped you all make a spiritual difference in your community?

A The theology of place helped us grow as both individuals and a church. One example is our discernment to even move locations and how this ties to our current hope and goals—to be rooted and established in love.

The process and story of [obtaining] our building is one that we [experienced] collectively as a church body. We prayed, discerned and worked together to purchase this building. We [knew] that with a move and rooting ourselves, God [might] change the demographics of our church. We believed that we would not merely "stumble" upon something—but rather, in our value of prayer, we sought God for him to tell us about the space, the stories, the people—and then we asked God, together, how we can partner with him. It was a slow and intentional process.

Since our move, our church has morphed and changed, and we believe it will continue to change into a church that God desires. This affects things that we say yes and no to with wisdom and discernment. It has also changed the way we show hospitality to our neighbors and those we find ourselves in close proximity to. This would not have occurred previously because we were in such a different context and space. We needed to be open to be changed. ●

CASE STUDY

A NEW WAY OF PARTNERING

Churches are large, community-driven buildings—but they often sit empty during the week. How can these spaces be leveraged and shared with the community in a way that's mutually beneficial?

ChurchSpace is answering this question by facilitating co-sharing opportunities for churches and their neighbors. Founded in 2019 by Day Edwards and Emmanuel Brown, the business has been described as "Airbnb for churches."

"As a two-sided marketplace, we help churches turn their underutilized real estate into on-demand commercial space for locals—connecting two groups that would have otherwise never met," Brown explains.

Brown and Edwards are both children of pastors and witnessed firsthand the challenges church leaders often face to maintain their congregations and their buildings.

"I served in my local church as the facilities and event director, and I realized that our church was struggling financially. I also did public relations for a lot of church leaders and realized they all had the same problem," Edwards tells Barna. "They were really struggling to make ends meet, but they all had these big, beautiful buildings."

Brown and Edwards see churches as essential to the vibrancy of a community, and ChurchSpace highlights the value of churches for "more than Sunday morning."

"The church is one of the few places in the community where people from different backgrounds, ethnicities, different occupations all come together in one place," Brown notes. "This can spur opportunities and create moments where those who live, partake and participate in the community can come together to strategize, 'What will make this community improve? What can make the community thrive?'—and do that through a Christ-centered lens."

From food truck events and sports leagues to community meetings and educational programs, ChurchSpace is an example of how churches can innovate and partner with others to bring new life to existing spaces.

"We've seen farmer's markets partner with churches through ChurchSpace where [organizers] say, 'There are no healthy options within the next 60-mile radius. How can we utilize your space to fulfill that need? How can we redeem that in a way that [is meaningful]?" Edwards says.

"Every community has a different need," she adds. And it's up to leaders to lean in and see how those needs can be met, perhaps through the use of church spaces.

For churches considering sharing or renting out their spaces, Brown and Edwards offer the following advice:

1. **Make the process seamless and special.** "You can open your space [for others to use] and think about the logistics and the operational process, but how do you make it a great experience for people who are coming into our space?" Brown asks. "You want to go above and beyond to make sure that people, when they walk into your space, they feel welcome, they feel attended to."

2. **Consistently invest in and beautify your spaces.** "Every church has character and value that can be used by its community," Brown reminds leaders. "Churches that have invested time and money into their space, we see them perform really well on our platform, as well as churches that have a deep desire to impact their community and this is [built into] their core values."

3. **Lean into the needs of your neighbors.** "Churches are deeply connected to the integrity and value of a community. When we invest in these assets, we can see the community grow and flourish leaps and bounds without always having to think of new [real estate] developments," Brown says.

Edwards adds that, "When churches share their space, they are actually increasing the economic value for those [they serve]. A small business owner doesn't have to drive across town [and enjoys a] reduced rate for office space. A chef who wants to expand to a different part of the city finds [a fitting] commercial kitchen space.

"Through a church space, the efforts of that person [and business] are poured back into the community and its economy." ●

A CHURCH WITH OPEN DOORS:
MAKING SPACE THROUGH COLLECTIVE COLLABORATION

Thoughts on church and community partnership from Elizabeth Howze, director of teaching, training & learning at Ormond Center

See page 10 to meet our contributors.

In order for congregations and communities to thrive in today's world, they must first cultivate a foundation of love, understanding and mutual respect for each other. When congregations learn to see and understand their community as living, breathing, complex ecosystems, they will become better suited to understand the multifaceted nature of the challenges their community faces—and be better equipped to cultivate thriving in their distinct context. These layered contextual understandings cannot be adequately uncovered in isolation and require congregations to build an appreciation for and mutually beneficial collaborations with community partners.

The local church is often one of the oldest institutions within a community. Because of this, they possess both tangible assets, such as property and financial resources, as well as intangible assets, such as extensive social memory and a level of communal trust. Additionally, when churches are ingrained into the DNA of communities, they can play a pivotal role in the formation of communal identity, values and codes of conduct.

Research shows that faith-based communities are long credited with innovative solutions across economic sectors that strengthen their local communities. Yet, many local congregations remain isolated from other congregations and community-facing organizations within their geographic regions.

We've learned that some of this isolation stems from fear of change and the unknown, limited opportunities to intentionally engage and build meaningful relationships with neighboring congregations and / or organizations, lack of innovative ideas, limited imagination and limited knowledge of how to bring about the impact or change that embodies their congregation's mission statement.

I would argue that it is a church community's ability to identify, leverage and mobilize their assets—seen and unseen—in creative and collaborative ways that will ultimately lead to faithful and just thriving for all.

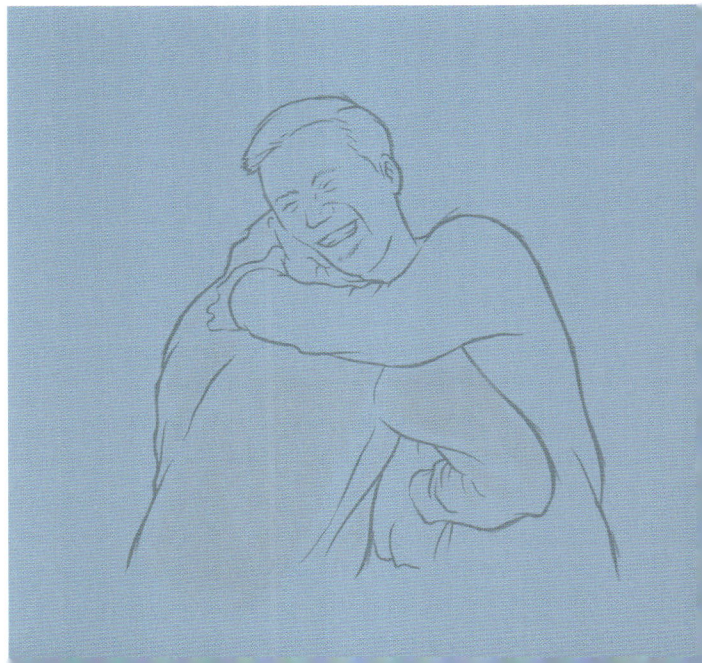

A GUIDE FOR CHURCH RENOVATION BUDGETING

In the planning process for how you might make better use of your church building, assessing the financial cost of designing and constructing a church space or facility is crucial. This is a step that causes many leaders *not* to move forward. But church buildings still matter today for both congregants and community. When done right, money spent on your church building is money spent on ministry.

Making Space data shows that pastors who are considering church building renovations in the next three years expect it to cost less than $1 million, indicating projects that are likely smaller in scale.

Still, those who give and tithe to the church are investing in the ministry of the church. When it comes to budgeting for your church build or renovation, clarity and transparency are key, especially considering most U.S. adults say they trust Christian churches with their financial support.[17]

It's also likely some church visitors will be keenly aware of how expensive (or not) your church space appears to be. While you can't control this, there are factors to consider, ensuring you're being a good steward.

Guidance & Best Practices

1. **Don't underestimate the complexities of a commercial build.** Someone with expectations formed by experience in residential architecture, interior design or construction will find themselves in a different ballpark when it comes to building for a church. The traditional process for establishing a budget is to create plans and then determine what they might cost. But with commercial builds, this can be a step too far and not far enough all at once. A simple concept is not sufficient to accurately determine costs, and designing scope without a budget in mind is a dangerous, often costly step. Partner with experts who understand this delicate balance and can help you navigate the scoping and budgeting process.

2. **Inspect first.** The costs of a renovation construction project can unfurl due to several factors like the age or condition of the existing building and what's needed or required to bring the building up to code. To get ahead of this, have the space thoroughly inspected and determine where maintenance or replacement is needed, as well as the required code compliance. Conducting a walk-through of the building with a professional *before* you start planning renovations can uncover hidden costs and barriers.

3. **Determine how you'll measure success.** The most expensive space a church can pay for is the *wrong* space for its congregants and community. This is why cost per square foot isn't

always the best measure of good stewardship. You might pay $100 per square foot for a 20,000-square-foot warehouse, or $400 per square foot for a 5,000-square-foot building that is furnished, hospitable and amenable for connection and discipleship. Either of these could be right, depending on your church's needs.

4. **Be aware of hidden costs.** Especially with a small renovation, there are important cost escalations to be careful to avoid. Expanding the footprint of a building usually triggers additional improvements, moving or replacing structural walls has a high price tag and large sitework projects can add up fast. In this same vein, cutting costs in some ways might end up costing more. For example, someone might—in good faith—volunteer labor, but the work may suffer in quality. In the long run, this may cost time, relationship capital and money.

5. **Embrace easy wins.** Curb-appeal projects, exterior improvements, art projects, landscaping, replacement materials and interior finishes can usually be improved or added on to a project without great infrastructure costs—and offer high yields.

CONCLUSION

MAKING SPACE FOR THE FUTURE CHURCH

Together, we are his house ... and the cornerstone is Christ Jesus himself.
We are carefully joined together in him, becoming a holy temple for the Lord.
—EPHESIANS 2:20–21 (NLT)

Inspiring, formative spaces give churches—and congregants—room to grow to their fullest potential. Throughout this series, we see how the design of a church's physical space can significantly influence the effectiveness of its ministry. After all, the church building facilitates the mission of a church and its core ministries. But there's more to the purpose of the church. Architect Kelvin Sampson describes it this way:

> [Churches] can be a practical resource for people's well-being, instrumental in transforming individual lives for the better. They are catalysts for community cohesion, influencing culture and facilitating all kinds of activities to meet people's social and spiritual needs. They demonstrate the long-term commitment of the local church to its community. A building says that the church is invested, available and here to stay.[18]

Making Space data show ways that the *form* of a church building is directly related to its *function*. Christians have the divine opportunity to welcome outsiders, usher peace, cultivate community and ultimately draw people into deep relationship and, community with God at the center. In essence, church buildings provide a platform and catalyst for connecting people with God and each other. Intentional design enhances this.

As you work to foster inspiration, community and formation in your building, let these statements guide you:

Point to God

With great detail, God gave the people of Israel instructions for designing the temple meant to glorify him. From the measurements and materials to guidance on who could enter the space and how, we see in scripture God's careful and meticulous nature. Then came Jesus, the physical manifestation of where God and humans meet. As Tim Keller once wrote, "Jesus was the temple to end all temples, the priest to end all priests and the sacrifice to end all sacrifices."[19]

Today's church, like the temple of ancient times, serves as a place to worship and experience God. It is also the place where the work of the Holy Spirit and the love of Christ is cultivated, to be exemplified in our day-to-day lives.

While spiritual formation doesn't exclusively happen in a church building, embodied worship and fellowship in church are powerful influences on a person's faith walk. We've seen in this research: A coffee shop, park or even a home cannot replace the sacredness and intentionality of a church building. It's this scaredness that people expect from a church. And Christians, as they are formed, increasingly want their church to point to God, not only in the explicit worship and teaching, but also in its appearance, how it makes them feel, and the subconscious ways they experience the space.

We see in the data that the most devoted Christians value community over a thought-provoking sermon. As Christians grow spiritually, so also grows the yearning to experience the peace and presence of God and demonstrate an active faith through practices like prayer, worship, discipleship and communion. Church is the place where these practices flourish.

Prioritize People

Religious architecture, human-scale design, Christian images, contemplative gardens, beautiful stained glass and even welcoming design are futile if what's done in the building doesn't spill over into the lives of those in the surrounding community. The church was created for worship. But worship was created for transformation.

"All buildings—whether art museums, gas stations, big-box retailers or churches—bear witness to the institutions they serve," writes David Gobel, architectural history professor at Savannah College of Art and Design. "Churches cannot ignore their civic role. The location, site planning, quality of materials, craftsmanship and design of a church building either contribute to or detract from the overall quality of the built environment of a community. Churches must consider, not only the architectural design of their buildings, but also their relationship to the streets, blocks and neighboring buildings of the surrounding community."[20]

We know that most U.S. adults—whether Christian or non-Christian, churched or unchurched, younger or older—agree churches have a responsibility to care for their community. The plurality of U.S. adults even go as far as to say the church *belongs* to the community it serves. Your church design strategy requires vision and leadership but also visible, lived-out care and concern for people.

Experience God's Work

Making space for the future Church means intentionally designing and adapting your church building (and the property it occupies) today to effectively advance the Kingdom for generations to come. This is no small task. But it is one that you'll never have to do alone. "I'd encourage all of you who are thinking about space not to race to the drawing board, but to the floorboard," says Al Gordon, rector of Saint Church. "Put your knees on the floor and ask God to build his house." As the spirit of God is reflected in your spaces, the work of God takes center stage. **Start making space today and see what God does.** ●

METHODOLOGY

Research for *Making Space* consists of data and analysis based on an online quantitative survey. This was a survey of 2,000 U.S. adults, conducted from February 28–March 9, 2022. The margin of error for the sample is +/- 2.0 percent at the 95 percent confidence level. For this survey, researchers used an online panel for data collection and observed a quota random sampling methodology. Quotas were set to obtain a minimum readable sample by a variety of demographic factors, and samples were weighted by region, ethnicity, education, age and gender to reflect their natural presence in the United States population (using U.S. Census Bureau data for comparison). ●

ACKNOWLEDGMENTS

Barna Group sincerely thanks our partners at Aspen Group, including Derek DeGroot, Elena Forsythe, Josh Gregoire, Becky Phillips, Lynn Pickard, Matt Rodgers, Marcos Rodriguez, Greg Snider and Jim Yeung, for their essential insight for the *Making Space* series. Your passion for this research, expertise in church design and commitment to fostering ministry through thoughtfully designed spaces has been invaluable throughout this effort.

We're also grateful for our generous contributors, whose voices and experiences enhanced the data. For this volume, we want to thank Emmanuel Brown, David Deeds, Day Edwards, Al Gordon, Jessica Gracewski, Elizabeth Howze, Duke Kwon, Ryan Moody, Matthew Niermann, Rachel Reed, Walt Roth, Michael Scheer, Elaine Schnabel, Heather Sibinski, David Taylor and Cynthia Wallace.

The Barna research team for this publication included Daniel Copeland, Ashley Ekmay and Chanté Smith. The editorial team included Cicely Corry, Elizabeth Laird and Alyce Youngblood. The church engagement team, who produced the corresponding *Making Space* podcast for this project, included Joe Jensen, Lauren Petersen and Layla Shahmohammadi. Douglas Brown edited the manuscript. Darius Corry illustrated the cover and interior page art. Annette Allen designed the interior layout and data visualizations. T'nea Rolle served as project manager. Brenda Usery managed production. Appreciation also goes to our Barna colleagues—Juli Cooper, Morgan Faasse, Jonathan Fawcett, Kelly Gordon, Mel Grabendike, Kristine Hampton, Savannah Kimberlin, David Kinnaman, Dr. Charlotte Marshall Powell, Matthew Randerson, Verónica Thames and Todd White—for their support on this unique project. ●

ENDNOTES

1   David Kinnaman, *You Lost Me* (Grand Rapids, MI: Baker Books, 2016).

2   Barna Group, *Aging Well* (Dallas: Barna Group, 2023).

3   Barna Group, "Two in Five Christians Are Not Engaged in Discipleship," January 26, 2022, https://www.barna.com/research/christians-discipleship-community/.

4   Duke Kwon, "The Tragedy to Communities When Church Building Are Demolished to Make Condos," *Washington Post*, March 28, 2018, https://www.washingtonpost.com/news/acts-of-faith/wp/2018/03/28/the-tragedy-to-communities-when-church-buildings-are-demolished-to-make-condos/.

5   David Kinnaman, "Rising Spiritual Openness in America," January 18, 2023, https://www.barna.com/research/rising-spiritual-openness/.

6   Samuel G. Candler, "What Makes a Place Sacred?" October 28, 2012, https://www.cathedralatl.org/sermons/what-makes-a-place-sacred/.

7   Matthew Lee Anderson, "Buildings Matter Because Bodies Matter ," *The Gospel Coalition*, July 6, 2011, https://www.thegospelcoalition.org/article/buildings-matter-because-bodies-matter/.

8   https://www.vanderbloemen.com/blog/civil-rights-to-present-day; video 5:05-5:33

9   John M. Perkins, *Dream with Me: Race, Love, and the Struggle We Must Win*, (Grand Rapids, MI: Baker Books, 2017).

10 Linda Patrick, "Why Church Buildings Matter Today," January 4, 2021, https://www.houseofgood.nationalchurchestrust.org/why-church-buildings-matter-today/.

11 Renee D. Goodwin *et al.*, "Trends in Anxiety Among Adults in the United States, 2008–2018: Rapid Increases Among Young Adults," *Journal of Psychiatric Research* 130 (November 2020) 441–446, https://www.ncbi.nlm.nih.gov/pmc/articles/PMC7441973/.

12 Barna Group, "New Data on Gen Z—Perceptions of Pressure, Anxiety and Empowerment," January 28, 2021, https://www.barna.com/research/gen-z-success/.

13 Greg Henrique, "The Core Need," June 25, 2014, https://www.psychologytoday.com/us/blog/theory-knowledge/201406/the-core-need.

14 John Stott, *The Living Church: Convictions of a Lifelong Pastor*, (Downer's Grove, IL: InterVarsity Press, 2007) 19–20.

15 Barna Group, "56% of Christians Feel Their Spiritual Life Is Entirely Private," March 16, 2022, https://www.barna.com/research/discipleship-friendship/.

16 Barna Group, "56% of Christians Feel Their Spiritual Life Is Entirely Private," March 16, 2022, https://www.barna.com/research/discipleship-friendship/.

17 Barna Group, *The Trust Factor: The State of Generosity* Series (Dallas: Barna Group, 2024).

18 Kingdom Bank, "Mission-shaped Buildings: Reimagining Church Architecture for Maximum Community Impact," (n.d.) https://www.kingdom.bank/mission-shaped-buildings-reimagining-church-architecture-for-maximum-community-impact/.

19 Timothy Keller, *The Prodigal God* (New York: Penguin Group, 2008) 16.

20 David Gobel, "Reforming Church Architecture," *The Gospel Coalition*, July 6, 2011, https://www.thegospelcoalition.org/article/reforming-church-architecture/.

ABOUT THE PARTNERS

Barna Group

In its 40-year history, Barna Group has conducted more than two million interviews over the course of thousands of studies and has become a go-to source for insights about faith and culture, leadership and vocation, and generations.

Barna Group has worked with thousands of businesses, nonprofit organizations and churches across the U.S. and around the world. Barna is an independent, privately held, nonpartisan organization based in Dallas, Texas, with offices in Nashville, Tennessee; Ventura, California; and Atlanta, Georgia.

barna.com

Aspen Group

Aspen Group is a ministry-focused design-build-furnish firm providing integrated solutions for church spaces, including additions, renovations and new builds. Aspen believes in designing purposeful church spaces that play a direct role in discipling people. The firm challenges the Church to think both practically and theologically while bringing the best of design and construction management to client projects. Aspen Group exists to create the new church architecture of our times, demonstrating the ministry impact of beautiful space.

aspengroup.com